W9-BXH-024

THE PROPHETS SPEAK

By the same author  THE OLD TESTAMENT SPEAKS

THE PROPHETS SPEAK

Law of Love— The Essence of Israel's Religion

By SAMUEL J. SCHULTZ

Harper & Row, Publishers
New York, Evanston, and London

FIRST EDITION

LIBRARY OF CONGRESS CATALOG CARD NUMBER: 68-10478

K-S

To My Parents
Who Taught Me to Revere God

CONTENTS

FOREWORD

COULD the Old Testament "God of wrath" be the same loving Father of whom Jesus spoke? Was Jesus' concept of a God of love revolutionary to the Jewish mind? Does the Old Testament represent *law* while the New Testament heralds the *age of grace?* Was the Mosaic law *annulled* or *fulfilled* by Jesus? In the following pages the author shares his consideration of these questions with the hope of stimulating more interest in the basic message of the prophets.

Addressed primarily to college and seminary students, pastors, and laymen who consider God's Word the infallible rule for faith and practice, this book focuses attention upon the central theme of the entire Bible—the law of love. This law was enunciated by Moses through whose writings the religion of Israel was revealed. Prophet after prophet emphasized the importance of man's love relationship with God and his fellow man. In the fullness of God's revelation Jesus Christ the Son came not only to restate the law of love but also to fulfill it. Through His teaching ministry Jesus exemplified a wholehearted devotion to God and then demonstrated His love for the human race through His redemptive death as God's righteous servant.

Out of this love relationship with both God His Father and man came Christ's new commandment to love one another.

Frequently the Old Testament is dismissed as mere legalism whereas, by contrast, the New Testament is regarded as a revelation of love and grace. If the prophets as spokesmen for God were recipients of divine revelation and if Jesus came as the fulfillment of that revelation, then the Old Testament provides the foundational background for the New Testament and the two should always be regarded as equally authoritative parts of the written Word of God.

This study of the law of love as announced by the prophets is based upon the biblical data as found in the unreconstructed text of the Bible. The author is keenly aware of the efforts of some nineteenth- and twentieth-century scholars to reconstruct the biblical text. The modern theories on which their reconstruction efforts are based are not necessarily true simply because they are widely accepted. It is reasonably well established that the Old Testament text in its unreconstructed form is the text upon which Jesus and His generation based their discussions.

One's basic presuppositions concerning the Scriptures crucially affect one's interpretation of the Old Testament. Significant in the study of the prophets' messages is the question whether Moses or Amos is to be considered the first great prophet. Once the Mosaic account as recorded in the Pentateuch is accepted in its present form rather than approached within the framework of reconstruction based on theories of some modern scholars, then the entire Old Testament is seen from a different perspective.

In this volume the author hopes to stimulate the serious student to study the Bible as a reliable and trustworthy text. The footnotes offer bibliographical data for more extensive study as related to modern scholarship. Especially helpful in providing insight and understanding were *Treaty of the Great King* by M. Kline and *Ancient Orient and Old Testament* by K. Kitchen. To my wife, Eyla June, and to my daughter Linda I am deeply indebted for their helpful suggestions in the preparation of this manuscript.

Wheaton, Illinois S.J.S.
May 9, 1968

I

PROPHETS IN THE OLD TESTAMENT

HEBREW prophets and their messages constitute the vital core of the literature known as the Old Testament. Consequently attention is repeatedly focused upon the historical setting of the prophets, the cultural and political context of their messages, and the relevance of prophetic books to the twentieth century.

PREVAILING VIEWS

Two major viewpoints currently prevail in Old Testament literature. The naturalistic perspective considers prophets and prophecy almost exclusively from the human vantage point, often ignoring and even obscuring any serious consideration of divine revelation and inspiration. The biblical approach uniquely emphasizes both the human and divine factors relating to the prophet and his message.

In the naturalistic interpretation, the prophets and their messages are merely regarded as normal developments in the religion of Israel.[1] Hebrew prophecy is considered as a political and social phenomenon. Prophets forged their messages out of contemporary developments and spoke to their people on the

[1] Norman H. Gottwald, *All the Kingdoms of the Earth* (New York: Harper & Row, 1964), pp. 45ff.

basis of keen insight and analysis of current events. The books in the Old Testament do not necessarily represent the writings of the prophets whose names they bear. Later editions of these writings reflect the work of anonymous writers so that the prophetic books assumed their present form at about 200 B.C.[2]

The book of Isaiah, by way of example, is frequently ascribed to (1) the eighth-century prophet Isaiah, chapters 1–39; (2) an anonymous writer known as Deutero-Isaiah, chapters 40–55; *ca.* 550 B.C.; and (3) a Trito-Isaiah who lived after 515 B.C. and wrote chapters 56–66. Even these three units are believed by present-day scholars to include many additions.[3] Daniel is not considered a prophet and the book bearing his name is second-century literature written during the Maccabean era.

The biblical approach to the prophets and their message considers supernatural as well as natural elements as essential for a comprehensive analysis. The Bible is regarded as a reliable primary source document for historical data concerning the prophets and their message. Prophets are men who were the recipients of messages given to them by God. The scriptural texts that assert that God spoke are taken seriously and not regarded as editorial insertions. Hundreds of these claims of divine authority occur throughout the Old Testament. God spoke to individuals and the message recorded is regarded as

[2] Johannes Lindblom, *Prophecy in Ancient Israel* (Philadelphia: Muhlenberg Press, 1963), asserts that the prophet is not primarily a creative thinker and advancing new insights but one who is overwhelmed by God in an ecstatic experience (pp. 105–219). He regards the narrative of the early prophets beginning with I Sam. 10:5 so filled with legendary material that it is difficult to reconstruct the historical facts with any degree of certainty. Cf. also *The Interpreter's Bible* for each of the prophetic books.

[3] T. Henshaw, *The Latter Prophets* (London: Allen & Unwin, 1958), pp. 111–36, 225–40, 255–65, cf. R. H. Pfeiffer, *Old Testament Introduction,* who attributes only about six chapters in Isa. 1–12 to the eighth-century prophet.

God's message when so identified in the scriptural text.[4] The contemporary milieu as known from the biblical text as well as from history and archeology is taken into account and related to the prophet and his message.[5]

The historical context as given in the Bible is likewise taken realistically. Moses is a prophet who lived during the fifteenth- to thirteenth-century era. He is not merely a "prophet" by retrojection but he was historically a man to whom God spoke.[6]

REVELATION—HUMAN AND DIVINE

Revelation involves events as well as their interpretation. While some writers today emphasize the acts of God, they continue to regard as of human origin the interpretation divinely given to Moses concerning God's manifestation of power during Israel's emancipation and migration.[7] Historically this interpretation was given to Moses, who conveyed its significance to the Israelites who participated in the exodus experience.[8]

[4] For a discussion of the Hebrew words indicating claims of authority, see A. B. Mickelsen, *Interpreting the Bible* (Grand Rapids, Mich.: Eerdmans, 1963), pp. 80–85. The prophetical as well as historical books repeatedly state "The utterance of Jehovah," "Thus says Jehovah, the God of Israel," "Jehovah speaks," or the "word of God" as an indication of divine authority.

[5] Cf. S. J. Schultz, *The Old Testament Speaks* (New York: Harper & Row, 1960), in discussion of the prophets.

[6] Cf. B. D. Napier, *Prophets in Perspective* (Nashville: Abingdon Press, 1962). The term "prophet" is ascribed to Moses by the E document, 850–750 B.C. and the D document from Josian times (pp. 61–64). The "historical Moses" and the "historical exodus" are irrecoverable, according to Napier.

[7] Note the analysis of this problem by Langdon B. Gilkey, "Cosmology, Ontology, and the Travail of Biblical Language," in the *Journal of Religion,* XL (1961), 200. For examples of current books where the acts of God are emphasized but the interpretation of the event is not explicitly regarded as part of divine revelation, see G. E. Wright and Reginald H. Fuller, *The Book of the Acts of God,* contemporary scholarship interprets the Bible (Garden City, N.Y.: Doubleday Anchor Books, 1960), and B. Anderson, *Understanding the Old Testament* (Englewood Cliffs, N.J.: Prentice-Hall, 1957).

[8] Cf. G. A. F. Knight, *Hosea* (London: SMC Press, 1960; Torch Bible

Another basic consideration for the interpretation of prophets and prophecy is the antiquity of the Pentateuch. Does the Pentateuch reflect the religion of Israel during Mosaic times or was the Pentateuch completed as a literary unit between 500 and 400 B.C. from the JEDP documents written in post-Davidic times?[9] According to the latter theory, Moses is regarded as a historical figure, but the literature relating to Moses is considered traditional and partly legendary, since it was committed to writing centuries later.[10] Although this documentary theory still dominates current Old Testament scholarship it is regarded as in a state of flux.[11] In recent decades numerous volumes on the prophets have been written from this perspective.[12] According to the documentary theory much of the Pentateuch was contemporary with and later than the prophets. Consequently the dating of the Pentateuch is crucial in the interpretation of prophetic literature.

Commentaries), p. 46, where he asserts that ". . . the significance of the exodus had been made plain by the prophetic bards and writers whom we call J and E, . . ."

[9] According to this theory the Pentateuch is composed of a great diversity of material reflecting Israel's pilgrimage from patriarchal times to the exile. Perhaps by about 950 B.C. a traditionalist from Judah organized the oral tradition in a written epic known as the J document. By 750 B.C. a traditionalist from the Northern Kingdom or Ephraim wrote his narrative version identified as the E document. The D document (Deuteronomy) was published in the seventh century. During the exile the priestly writers wrote the P document with material preserved by the Jerusalem priesthood. By 400 B.C. these documents were combined into one literary unit known as the Pentateuch and attributed to Moses.

[10] R. B. Y. Scott, *The Relevance of the Prophets* (New York: The Macmillan Co., 1944), pp. 59ff.

[11] Cf. John Bright, "Old Testament Criticism," ch. 1 in *The Bible and the Ancient Near East*, ed. G. E. Wright (1958).

[12] Note the recent publication by B. D. Napier, *Prophets in Perspective* (Nashville: Abingdon Press, 1962); also *The Interpreter's Bible* and Torch Bible commentaries.

THE MOSAIC LEGACY

The Mosaic authorship of the Pentateuch has much in its favor. As a result of archeological knowledge the Pentateuchal tradition is regarded as substantially Mosaic in character.[13] From the literary standpoint the book of Deuteronomy compares more favorably with fifteenth-century documents than with seventh-century writings.[14] The biblical data point to Mosaic authorship. Moses himself was intimately associated with all the events in the Pentateuch beginning with Exodus. The rest of the Bible, both Old and New Testaments, ascribes the Pentateuch to Moses. A recent analysis, which supports the literary unity of the Pentateuch, points to Moses as its author.[15] Evidence from the ancient Near East supports not only the possibility that Moses *could* write but also the probability that he *did* write. Important documents were written down and then made known widely to contemporaries by means of oral tradition. Moses deposited the law by the Ark (Deut. 31:9) and instructed the Israelites to read it publicly (Deut. 31:11).[16] Thus by means of oral dissemination the Israelites were to be familiarized repeatedly with what God had revealed to him concerning their pattern of living.

[13] Wm. F. Albright, *The Archaeology of Palestine* (Penguin Books, 1949).

[14] Meredith Kline, *Treaty of the Great King* (Grand Rapids: Eerdmans, 1963).

[15] Gleason L. Archer, *A Survey of Old Testament Introduction* (Chicago: Moody Press, 1964).

[16] K. A. Kitchen, in *The New Bible Dictionary,* ed. J. D. Douglas (London: Inter-varsity Fellowship, 1962), in his articles entitled "Egypt," pp. 347–53, and "Moses," pp. 843–50, points out that evidence from the ancient Near East supports the thesis that nearly the whole body of material in the Pentateuch could have been arranged in its present form as early as Joshua with a minimum of later orthographic and linguistic revisions. Oral transmission was primarily used for contemporary dissemination of written materials.

If the law deposited by the Ark was the Pentateuch then this body of literature served as the basis for the messages of the prophets. The religious ideal for the Israelites was in written form and disseminated to successive generations. Amos, as an example, makes numerous references to the law but does not offer evidence that he was pioneering in new theological ideas or crusading for a new moral code.[17] His appeal was based on Israel's knowledge of the law of Moses.

Pivotal to the entire consideration of the prophets and their message is the recognition of Moses as the first great prophet in Israel's historical background. Whether Moses actually was a prophet as the Bible projects him or was merely "called a prophet by later men of prophetic lineage" is basically significant.[18] Did prophecy begin with Moses or did Hebrew prophecy come from Canaanite contact?[19] Did Moses lead twelve tribes out of Egypt or is this only an impression created by the fusing of the various documents in the Pentateuch?[20] Did God reveal himself to Moses or is the burning-bush experience merely a story ascribed to Moses in later tradition? Was the law actually given to Moses by God or does it merely exemplify the creative genius of Moses? Are the tabernacle, the offerings, and the feasts and seasons as outlined in the Pentateuch realistically associated with Moses or are they later inventions by the Priestly writers?

If Moses is taken seriously as a prophet through whom the basic truths of Israel's religion were revealed as recorded in the Pentateuch then the ministry of the prophets is basically of

[17] Archer, *op. cit.*, pp. 307–8. Cf. also J. G. S. S. Thomson in "Amos," in *The New Bible Dictionary.*

[18] Scott, *op cit.*, p. 51. Deut. 18:15, 18 is considered as part of the D document written in the sixth century B.C.

[19] Gottwald, *op. cit.*, p. 49.

[20] H. H. Rowley, *The Missionary Message of the Old Testament* (London: Carey Kingsgate Press, 1944), p. 12.

a supplementary nature. Israel's responsibility and purpose were clearly delineated by Moses. Prophets came to remind successive generations of the truth expressed in the written law as it applied to the contemporary condition. Additional revelation which was given to the prophets was always in harmony with the law. As each prophet recorded his own message he contributed to the sacred literature which told of God's dealings with the Israelites. God's message to His people in Old Testament times became more complete in the coming of the God-man Christ Jesus. In this way the fullness of divine truth was progressively revealed. Throughout the centuries from the beginning of the human race to the coming of Christ the redemptive purpose of God was communicated to mankind.

Prophets and their messages need to be considered in their historical background. Their messages become relevant today only as the significance for the times in which they were given is correctly understood. Basic principles pertaining to the relationship between God and man are as vital today as they were when the prophet uttered them.

II

CITIZENS WITH GOD'S MESSAGE

THE PROPHET has a very significant place throughout the Old Testament. From Moses to Malachi, prophets are active in Israel, making a vital contribution through their impact upon contemporary developments.

What the prophet actually did and who he was can best be ascertained from the biblical context. Although the Scriptures do not offer a biographical account of each prophet, enough cumulative data are given to indicate the essential distinctives that characterize a prophet in Israel.

Moses is significantly identified as the great prophet of Old Testament times (Hos. 12:13). Fortunately more is known about Moses as the prophet through whom Israel's religion was initially revealed than any other prophet in the Old Testament Scriptures. Furthermore the literature that contains his messages and what was revealed through him exceeds that of the later prophets. From the birth of Israel as a nation Moses was personally involved in delivering the Israelites from Egyptian bondage and establishing them as an independent nation. Through him was revealed the significance of the exodus, the law and the covenant, the provisions for building the tabernacle, the instructions for observing the feasts and seasons, civil regulations and finally an elaboration of the laws and instructions for the occupation of Canaan.

CHARACTERISTICS OF A PROPHET

With Moses as the example, the earmarks of Old Testament prophets became apparent.[1] A careful study of the historical context of subsequent prophets offers a fuller understanding of the essential characteristics of a true prophet.

A Divine Call

God took the initiative in the making of a prophet. No true prophet assumed his ministry as a vocational choice or on his own initiative. A prophet who was not divinely called was a false prophet and consequently came under God's condemnation (Jer. 14:14; 23:21). A prophet was not appointed by a king, a priest, elders, or by popular choice.

No particular vocational training was necessary for prophetic candidacy to be a prophet. God called men from varied vocations and backgrounds. The training and preparation for a prophetic ministry also varied. Moses had an extensive education in the Egyptian court whereas Amos did not have any formal training although he does reflect considerable knowledge of the Mosaic law.

Nor did a prophet come into his office by reason of birth. None of the writing prophets was the son of a prophet; nor were they succeeded in their ministries by any of their sons. The call to be a prophet came by divine choice and was not prescribed by any human standards or regulations.

[1] The word *nabi* in Exod. 7:1 identifies a man who is a spokesman for another—Aaron spoke for Moses and Moses spoke for God (cf. Exod. 4:15–17). This idea is confirmed in Deut. 18:15–22 where the prophet arising after Moses is one who will speak for God.

The divine call made the individual conscious of being in the presence of God. Moses became aware of God's nearness through the burning bush (Exod. 3–4). He was not left to his own resources to explain this phenomenon of a flame of fire. Through a divine revelation its significance was evident as God broke the silence and made Moses conscious of the presence of a holy God. The fact that God was calling Moses was so explicitly clear that Moses never had any doubt about his divine encounter. Subsequently he spoke with certainty to Aaron (Exod. 4:28), to the Israelites (Exod. 6:9), and even to pharaoh (Exod. 5:1) about the fact that God had called him to his mission of delivering the Israelites from Egyptian bondage.

During the course of his ministry the Israelites contested the divine call of Moses. Repeatedly God confirmed to Moses and to the Israelites that He had called him to his place of leadership and responsibility (Num. 12:6–8; 16:28). His role as a prophet was not dependent upon any delegation or committee from the Israelite nation but was of divine appointment.

God used various means of making a prophet conscious of His presence. Samuel became cognizant of God's presence as he heard a voice which he acknowledged as a divine call to be a prophet in Israel (I Sam. 3:3). Isaiah may have been in the environs of the temple as he became keenly aware that a holy God was commissioning him to be His messenger (Isa. 6). Jeremiah does not offer any details but he simply states that God was speaking to him (Jer. 1). Throughout his book he reaffirms the fact that he was called by God to be a prophet. Ezekiel seems to have had the most elaborate and extensive manifestation of God's presence (Ezek. 1–3). Coming from a priestly family and possibly having been reared in the environs of the temple of Jerusalem, Ezekiel may have needed such a vision to make him aware of God's presence in the midst of a pagan Babylonian environment. This divine encounter made Ezekiel cognizant of his prophetic mission among the Israelite exiles. Amos does not give any details about his call but does definitely reflect the fact that God spoke to him, and subsequently he could not resist giving forth God's message (Amos 3:8). Many prophets do not record their calls, but the evidence for their divine commission is apparent in their ministry.

The consciousness of being in the presence of God and hearing an explicit commission from a holy God constitutes a divine call. Without this a man could not be a prophet. Initiated by God, this divine encounter marked the beginning of a prophet's career as it did, for example, in the life of Moses. This divine call was specific and personal.

A Message from God

Another distinctive characteristic of a prophet was the fact that he had a God-given message. The impartation of this message was divinely initiated and not precipitated by the prophet seeking revelational contact or achieving an ecstatic state or frenzy.[2] The initial message was usually imparted when the prophet was called to communicate a message for God to man.

The message God gave to Moses was explicitly clear. Conscious of the Israelites' oppression in Egypt, God promised that they would be freed from servitude. Moses was commissioned to announce this message to pharaoh as well as to the Israelites (Exod. 3:10, 16). Such a message was unpleasant for the former, whereas for the Israelites it provided optimism and hope. The acts of God associated with the deliverance of the Israelites were frequently accompanied by divine interpretation.

[2] For the view that the prophets of Israel were ecstatics seeking divine contacts even as the Canaanites did, see John Bright, *History of Israel* (Philadelphia: Westminster Press, 1959), p. 166; H. Knight, *The Prophetic Consciousness* (London: Lutterworth Press, 1947), pp. 80–81; H. H. Rowley, *The Faith of Israel* (London: SMC Press, 1956), pp. 37–39.

The death of the firstborn, by way of example, was preceded by instructions for all Israelites to participate in the observance of the Passover. Consequently they were not left to their own resources in seeking an explanation after this miraculous act of God occurred, but they were divinely instructed through Moses concerning its significance before God's judgment was executed.

The particular messages varied with each prophet. For Samuel the divine communication involved specific judgment upon the leading family in Israel to whom religious as well as civic responsibilities were entrusted. For Isaiah and Jeremiah it meant the announcement of judgment upon Judah. They were sent to a sinful people who were falling short of God's requirements. Judgment was imminent and the prophets were commissioned to announce the impending doom. Both of these prophets, however, also had messages of hope and assurance.

Although the content of the divinely given messages varied, the significant fact is that each man who was called by God was also given a specific message. God's revelation to each prophet had a content that was related to the particular time and place in which the prophet lived. The communication was relevant to the situation, had a bearing on current events, and was significant for the people to whom it was delivered.

A Spokesman for God

Uniquely characteristic of the prophets was the fact that they spoke for God. Sent by God with a specific message they represented Him to the people. Whereas the function of a priest was to represent the people before God, the prophet was called to take God's place before his fellow men. In this sense a prophet bridged the gap between God and man. He was the medium through whom God communicated to the human race.

When the prophet conveyed this message it was authoritative. Divine in its origin, this word was binding in the divine-human relationship. The authority rested in God and not in the prophet. The latter was only the spokesman for God.

In the account of the call and experience of Moses it is explicitly delineated that the prophet is a spokesman for God. Moses was keenly conscious of the authority wielded by the pharaoh of Egypt. Having grown up in the royal court of the most advanced center of civilization and the leading seat of international power in the Fertile Crescent, Moses realized that the ruler of Egypt would not be disposed to release the Israelites at his request. With reason Moses raises the question of authority and in response God assumes him of His divine presence. When Moses and Aaron deliver the message to pharaoh it is prefaced by "thus saith the Lord God of Israel" (Exod. 5:1). In the course of negotiations this authority is made more vivid when God assures Moses, ". . . see, I have made thee a god to Pharaoh; and thy brother shall be thy prophet" (Exod. 7:1). In his encounter with pharaoh Moses experienced an awareness that he himself could not command the king of Egypt but was dependent upon the God for whom he spoke.

Moses realized that his word alone would not be respected even among his own people. To the Israelites he is commanded to speak for the "I AM" or the God who appeared to Abraham, Isaac, and Jacob. The eternal God who made the promises to the patriarchs is speaking through Moses. Repeatedly Moses in his role as leader of Israel conveys what God revealed to him with the preface, "Thus saith the Lord." Speaking for God he continued to communicate what was divinely revealed to the Israelites, guiding them in their national emergence.

Divine Enabling

A true prophet was assured of supernatural enablement to carry out his mission. God's call to an individual to be His representative also included the assurance of supernatural resources. The assistance or intervention of divine power was sufficient to accomplish God's purpose even though the individual was not fully aware of God's plan for him.

Moses as a spokesman for God was given a more complex and difficult assignment than any other prophet. He faced a generation of unbelieving Israelites as well as the powerful king of Egypt. To his own people Moses appealed on the basis of the divine promises made to their forefathers, but even then they were not aware of the mighty acts of God in their behalf. To pharaoh "the Lord God of the Hebrews" (Exod. 9:1) had no significance. His initial reaction and reply was, "Who is the Lord, that I should obey his voice to let Israel go? I know not the Lord, neither will I let Israel go" (Exod. 5:2). From the human standpoint Moses had been given an assignment that was impossible to fulfill.

For the Israelites, God's provision for Moses was designed to provide a reasonable basis for their faith. Having no resources of his own with which to help his people or even to accredit himself before them, Moses was receptive to God's supernatural aid. The signs of the leprous hand and the serpents were given him to gain the support of his own people. The subsequent manifestation of divine intervention provided additional evidence of God's provision for them.

To pharaoh and the Egyptians the plagues came as a demonstration of the power of the Hebrew God. Through this series of plagues, judgment was executed upon the gods of Egypt. Pharaoh in the course of these events was convinced that he was confronted with a power he could not control or equal. Through the experience of the plagues he became acquainted with the God of the Hebrews. Though Moses appeared in person before pharaoh it became evident that Moses had resources beyond his own. In this way miracles enabled Moses to be an effective spokesman for God.

The interpretation of these mighty acts of God was also given to and through Moses. He was not left to an analysis of these events from the human perspective. Significant is the fact that the meaning of these events was divinely revealed before the mighty acts of God were witnessed by men.

Initially in God's commission to Moses the fact is plainly stated that God is going to deliver the Israelites (Exod. 3). Moses from time to time explains that God will do signs and wonders. Consequently the plagues did not merely fall into the category of destructive manifestations in nature, such as tornadoes, hurricanes, and floods, but came as the result of a divine plan and purpose as revealed through Moses. Both the Egyptians and the Israelites were to have an experience whereby they would know God as they had never known Him before. Through their deliverance from Egyptian bondage the Israelites were to "know that I am the Lord your God" and realize that God by His mighty hand was intervening for them (Exod. 6:7). Although the Egyptians were mighty (Exod. 3:19) and did not fear God (Exod. 9:30), the purpose of the plagues was clearly explained by Moses before they came. Pharaoh was "to know" or learn through this supernatural demonstration "that the earth is the Lord's" (Exod. 9:29).

The meaning of the judgment in the death of the firstborn and the institution of the Passover was explicitly made plain through Moses before these events came to pass. These mighty acts, which climaxed the entire series of God's demonstrations of power, brought judgment upon the Egyptians and deliverance for all who believed Moses and obeyed the instructions to observe the Passover. Before the last plague a timely warning was given so that all who were secluded behind blood-covered doorposts might be spared divine judgment.

The scriptural context is elaborate enough to assert that the institution of the Passover was uniquely revealed to Moses rather than adapted from Egyptian festivals. Moses was God's spokesman and leader through whom God's purpose in delivering Israel was accomplished.

Prophets subsequent to Moses were likewise assured of divine enabling. Samuel, leading his people in a spiritual revival, assured them of victory over the Philistines. After gathering for prayer at Mizpah, the Israelites defeated the advancing enemy as God's mighty power was displayed in their behalf (I Sam. 7). Isaiah was assured of divine enabling through a divine touch that cleansed him from his sin so he could serve as God's representative to his generation (ch. 6). Jeremiah, keenly aware of the opposition he would face in announcing the doom of Jerusalem, was assured of divine protection throughout his ministry (ch. 1). In an encounter with the false prophet Hananiah, Jeremiah and his audience witnessed the confirmation of his message through the fulfillment of his prediction. Hananiah's death as predicted should have convinced the Israelites that Jeremiah was divinely enabled (ch. 28). Ezekiel likewise was divinely empowered and established as God's spokesman in his responsibility as a watchman to the house of Israel in Babylonia. God's abandonment of the temple as proclaimed by Ezekiel, beginning in 593 B.C., was literally fulfilled by 586 B.C. when Jerusalem was razed by the Babylonians.

Accountability to God

A prophet was directly responsible to God. Being divinely called to service, given a message to deliver, and endowed with supernatural resources to accomplish his mission, a true representative of God was accountable to God for his ministry. He was not to be influenced by the people, nor was he to modify his message. Regardless of the circumstances, political pressure, or religious climate, the prophet was a man whom God held responsible to communicate the divinely given message. A distinctive mark of a prophet was a genuine consciousness that he was accountable to God as His representative.

Moses exemplified this sense of accountability. Whether he stood before the pharaoh of Egypt or faced his own unbelieving people he made it very clear that he himself was under God's directive. When the Israelites faced the Red Sea, with the Egyptians pursuing them, Moses appealed to God in this apparently hopeless situation. Divine aid was manifested in Israel's salvation and the drowning of the enemy. When Moses' leadership was contested repeatedly—by Miriam and Aaron (Num. 12), by Dathan, Korah, and Abiram, or the entire congregation (Num. 13–18)—Moses was divinely confirmed through various miraculous acts as he acknowledged that he was accountable to God. Significant is the incident where Moses lapsed in his sense of accountability (Num. 20:1–13). Failing to speak to the rock as bidden, he smote the rock in unbelief and subsequently suffered the consequences.

Ezekiel is another notable example of an Old Testament prophet's accountability to God. He is emphatically impressed with his responsibility as a watchman to the house of Israel. Regardless of the response and attitude of this audience he is accountable to God for communicating the message entrusted to him (chs. 1–3). Even if the people ignore his warning, he will deliver his own soul only by obeying God's command.

Contemporary Recognition

Another earmark of a prophet was the recognition that he was a man of God. Sent by God, the prophet normally had a ministry to the generation in which he lived. Acknowledgment by the people that this man was God's representative is usually evident in some form or another. Endorsement or recognition by the crowd was not always essential. Sometimes this acknowledgment came from a faithful few or from the populace at large. At other times a prophet was so recognized by an enemy, who might seek revenge so that the prophet suffered persecution or even martyrdom.

When Moses appeared before pharaoh of Egypt he was in time acknowledged as a representative of God. At first pharaoh refused to recognize Moses as a spokesman for God, but as the pressure of the plagues intensified the king of Egypt, recognizing that Moses had an audience with God, pleaded with Moses to intercede for him.

Samuel was so effective in his ministry that all Israel from Dan to Beersheba accorded him recognition as a prophet. In contrast to the laxity and apostasy that prevailed in Israel as Eli performed the ritual forms of Israel's religion, the spiritual leadership of Samuel made the entire nation aware that here was a man of God. Both Saul and David accorded him this recognition.

In Davidic times Nathan and Gad were duly recognized as messengers of God. Even though they came with reproof for the king, it was apparent to David that these men were spokesmen for God. Among many others who were acknowledged by their contemporary generations to be God's prophets were Ahijah, Elijah, Micaiah, Elisha, Amos, and Isaiah. To enemies as well as friends it was apparent that these men were sent by God with a message which was relevant to the time in which they lived.

Titles

"Man of God" is commonly used as a general title for a prophet in Old Testament times, beginning with Moses in Deut. 33:1. Men representing God were not always identified by their given names. Notable examples of this are the prophet who warned Eli (I Sam. 2:27ff.), and the prophet from Judah who rebuked King Jeroboam in Bethel (I Kings 13). Elisha is designated as a "holy man of God" in II Kings 4:9.

A general title from the divine perspective was the commonly used word "servant." Again Moses is the first one so identified (Josh. 1:2). Among other references, where men who were divinely commissioned to represent God were identified as God's servants, are II Kings 17:13, 23; 21:10; 24:2; Ezra 9:11; Jer. 7:25.

The Hebrew word most frequently used throughout the Old Testament to identify a prophet is *nabi*.[3] Beginning with Exod. 7:1, the idea repeatedly associated with a true prophet is that he conveys a divinely given message and consequently is a spokesman for God. Isaiah (6:9), Jeremiah (1:7), and Ezekiel (2:3–4) are explicitly commissioned to speak for God. The Hebrew words *ro'eh* and *hozeh* signify the activity of a seer or one who sees. Samuel, Gad, and others who are identified as

[3] The verb corresponding to the noun *nabi* is *hithnabbe*, meaning "to prophesy." In Amos 7:12–16 the meaning of this word in the context pointedly indicates that Amos the prophet was prophesying when he was speaking God's message. In its noun and verb forms this Hebrew word occurs over 300 times primarily related to preaching a message.

In some instances the verb "to prophesy" involves the idea "to praise," as is apparent in I Chron. 25:1–3. This may also have been the activity described in Num. 11:25–29, I Sam. 10:1–13, and I Sam. 19:18–24. In none of these references is there any indication that a divine revelation occurred in which a new message from God was given to the participants.

In two references "to prophesy" may mean "to rave" or "to act violently" (cf. I Sam. 18:10 and I Kings 18:29). In neither case is a message given, but violent activity is indicated. Leon J. Wood, "Ecstasy and Israel's Early Prophets," *Bulletin of the Evangelical Theological Society*, IX (1966), 125–37, points out that in all the references above, where no giving of a message is involved, the activity described is "not basically intellectual but emotional." Applying these secondary meanings of "praising" and "raving" to the basic idea of "speaking a message," Wood concludes that "to prophesy" in its full sense means "to speak fervently." Says Wood in his conclusion, "The prophet if he spoke in character as a true prophet spoke with emotion. He put his heart into his message. He proclaimed with strength. He did not recite words but preached a message."

seers are known for their activity in proclaiming God's message. All three Hebrew words suggest the basic idea that people so identified were spokesmen for God.

CHARACTERISTICS OF THE MESSAGE

The prophet's mission and message were usually relevant to the generation and the particular circumstances in which he lived. Being a man of his time he usually had an awareness of contemporary events and developments. Divinely moved, he communicated his message with its bearing on personal, national, or international affairs at that particular time. Neither the prophet nor his message was isolated from his contemporary world.

Concern with Spiritual Relationships—The Law of Love

Of primary concern to the prophet was the law of love in the relationship between God and man. Through Moses, God manifested himself to the Israelites by their deliverance from Egypt. Through mighty acts and their God-given interpretation, the Israelites became experientially aware of the covenant relationship existing between them and their God. According to the book of Deuteronomy, Moses renewed the covenant with the new generation before his death, emphasizing primarily the law of love. Although this consciousness of a divine-human relationship was to be a vital reality in each succeeding generation through the observance of the Passover and other festivals, the human tendency toward apostasy was frequently evident in Israel. Message after message as exemplified by the prophets was designed to renew this relationship. Hosea, by way of example, extensively develops this theme of the Israelites' lack of love and of the knowledge of God. Intellectually well versed in theology, these people did not live as though they respected, revered, and loved God, nor were they concerned about putting into practice in daily life what was pleasing to God. They had failed to observe the law of love toward God as well as toward their fellow men.

An awareness of history was likewise apparent in the prophetic messages. This stemmed from Moses, who related all the events of the exodus, the experiences in the wilderness, and the prospects of conquering and living in Canaan to the Lord of history. Message after message was delivered in subsequent periods reminding the Israelites of the past with a keen sensitivity to the historic significance of the present.

Several prophets speak of Israel's relationship with God in terms of matrimony (Isa. 50:4; Jer. 3; Ezek. 23; Hos. 1–3). God was married to Israel, but the latter had broken her vows. Frequently the unfaithfulness of Israel was portrayed, pointing to the terrible deeds that had destroyed this unique matrimonial bond between Israel and her God.

Based on the Law of Moses

The requirements prescribed in the Mosaic revelation provided a normal frame of reference for the prophets subsequent to the time of Moses. The prophets did not concern themselves with the minute details or with the legalistic aspects of the law. Idolatry was the most prevalent offense among the Israelites. Instead of loving God wholeheartedly, they repeatedly turned to idols and consequently diverted their affection from God. This was the breaking of the first and greatest of all commandments. As long as this condition of misplaced devotion existed, the observance of the rest of the law was worthless and ineffective in their relationship with God. The ritual of the formal worship of God in the temple or at the altar of sacrifice could not be synchronized in any manner pleasing to God. As far as the prophets were concerned, little else mattered when the first commandment was broken.

The ethical and social concern expressed by Moses was likewise repeatedly appealed to by the prophets. Having departed from the prescribed Mosaic standard, the Israelites were warned by the prophets of their shortcomings on the basis of the divinely revealed law of Moses. Love for their fellow men was lacking because they failed in their love for God.

The prophets frequently rebuked the people and announced the impending judgment. Moses in the Deuteronomic renewal of the covenant warned his people that a failure in their commitment to God would result in divine disfavor and exile. Prophets subsequently pointed out that disobedience to God's requirements would bring the destruction of Jerusalem and exilic conditions.

The counterpart to this message of judgment was the hope of restoration. This likewise had been given by Moses in his final message before his death (Deut. 28–30). Prophets directed their reminders of judgment to the wicked people in order to spur them on to repentance. The message of hope and restoration provided comfort and assurance to those who put their trust and confidence in God as they expressed a concern to live as God's holy people.

Additional Revelation

Progressive revelation was another earmark of the prophetic message. During the entire Old Testament era, God was revealing Himself more fully to mankind until the full revelation came in Jesus Christ. Additional truths were usually related to that which had been made known previously. When God spoke to Moses, the promises made to Abraham, Isaac, and Jacob were brought into focus. Revelation to and through Moses was supplementary to and in harmony with the divine commitments made to the patriarchs. In turn the prophets following Moses projected their messages in harmony with the written law

(Deut. 13:5), and additional truth was revealed from time to time. In the light of the particular circumstances in which the prophet spoke, new insights and added information were made known to provide a fuller understanding of God's plan of redemption. Through Nathan in a time of national prosperity and political success was projected the promise and hope of an eternal succession on the throne of David. Later, more details were given through other prophets.

Foretelling the Future

Prediction was frequently characteristic of the prophet's message. It constituted a basic part of that which God revealed to Moses initially. God's specific promise was that the Israelites would be delivered from Egypt and established in the land of Canaan. This prediction was only partially fulfilled under Moses' leadership. It was tempered in its immediate fulfillment by the disobedience of the unbelieving Israelites at Kadesh-barnea, but Moses confidently assured his people that it would be fulfilled after his death under the leadership of Joshua. Moses also predicted the exile of Israel but with its ultimate restoration. Whereas the Israelites were frequently subjected to godless and wicked kings even on the Davidic throne, the prophetic messages provided the promise of a righteous ruler who would ultimately reign universally.

This predictive element was normal to the message of a prophet. Because his message had its origin with God, it was to be expected that future events would be included, since the past, present, and future were all known to the eternal, omniscient, and omnipotent God. Even though the predictive element was not the primary or the dominant part of the prophetic message, it was not the least of the characteristics that made the phenomenon of Israelite prophecy unique.

III

MOSAIC RELIGION

THE HEART of the religion of Israel is the covenant between God and Israel as revealed and established through Moses. Unique in its significance it provides the core of Old Testament revelation which was supplemented by the prophets in subsequent generations until it was culminated in the person of Jesus Christ.

Moses was the mediator of the covenant. All too often he has been primarily portrayed as the great lawgiver, and the Old Testament has been regarded as the deposit of a "legal religion" at the heart of which was the law, or the Decalogue.[1] Often the Ten Commandments have been projected in isolated form as the core of Mosaic revelation, obscuring the greater context of the covenant in which they were given. It was not obedience to the law that resulted in the establishment of the covenant. God miraculously delivered Israel out of Egypt and then made the covenant, which was followed by His ordinances providing

[1] Martin Luther came very near to identifying the Old Testament with God's law and the New Testament with the gospel according to G. von Rad, *Old Testament Theology* (New York: Harper & Row, 1965), Vol. II, p. 389. Cf. also H. Bornkamm, *Luther und das Alte Testament* (Tübingen, 1948), pp. 103ff., and G. Heintze, *Luthers Predigt von Gesetz und Evangelium* (Munich, 1958).

guidance in maintaining this relationship.[2] In the strict theological sense the commandments were not "law," since they lacked the positive completeness which normally is expected in a code and were predominantly negative.[3] Nor did the commandments outline a complete ethical code. They did, however, indicate the minimum that would be expected of one who was in a covenant relationship with a holy God. Consequently these commandments, ordinances, and laws should be considered subsidiary in the greater covenant relationship existing between God and Israel.

In the biblical context, the covenant was not an innovation. After the flood, God established a covenant with Noah (Gen. 9:13–16). To Abraham, the divine covenant provision was unfolded in a progressive revelation (Gen. 12–25), to which he responded in faith and obedience.[4] The content of these promises was passed on through the patriarchal line to the Israelites in Egypt.

At Mount Sinai the Mosaic covenant was established (Exod. 20–31). Although broken by the idolatry of the Israelites under Aaron (Exod. 32–33), it was immediately renewed under Moses' leadership (Exod. 34). After the Israelites were subjected to thirty-eight years of wandering, during which the un-

[2] For discussion see Walther Zimmerli, *The Law and the Prophets* (New York: Harper & Row, 1965), p. 47.

[3] For a discussion of the *paraclesis* in Deuteronomy—often called *paranesis*—see G. von Rad, *op. cit.*, pp. 393–94. See also Vol. I (1962), p. 194.

[4] G. E. Mendenhall, "Covenant Forms in Israelite Tradition," *Biblical Archaeologist*, XVII (September, 1954), 62, and David Freedman, "Divine Covenants and Human Obligation," *Interpretation*, XVIII (October, 1964), 419–31, consider that Abram had no obligation in the covenant God made with him, so that the Mosaic covenant differs from it in that the Israelites were obligated in return. Meredith Kline, *Treaty of the Great King* (Grand Rapids: Eerdmans, 1963), pp. 22–23, points out that Abram by rebellion would have forfeited the divine promise (Gen. 22:16–27a; cf. Deut. 28:63ff.).

believing generation died, the covenant was renewed with the new generation as Moses orally set before them the terms of the covenant (Deut. 1:1–32:47). Under the leadership of Joshua this covenant was once again renewed. Subsequently the prophets assumed this covenant-form in historical retrospect in their controversy pattern. They acknowledged that national destruction came because the Israelites had defied the God with whom they had a covenantal relationship and that they had deliberately violated and broken the terms of the covenant.[5] The Mosaic covenant provided the basic framework for the religion of Israel throughout Old Testament times. Although prophets supplemented the Mosaic revelation, making it relevant to their contemporary generations, it was never negated or replaced by them. It provided the foundation for national and individual success.

THE HISTORICAL CONTEXT

Current scholarship is giving more realistic consideration to the historical context of the biblical account of the Mosaic covenant. Recent studies in the light of archeological penetration into the contemporary culture of Old Testament times have offered factual data to invalidate prevailing theories.

Wellhausen's proposal that the covenant was developed by the people under the stimulating influence of the prophets, beginning with the eighth century, permeated Old Testament scholarship around the turn of the twentieth century.[6] Further-

[5] Freedman, *op. cit.,* p. 428, correctly points out that under the terms of the covenant each Israelite had a dual responsibility of obedience to the ordinances that applied to him and to participate in the orderly administration of equity and justice in the community.

[6] Wellhausen adopted the thesis of Graf who projected the theory that the law was later than the prophets. In his book *Geschichte Israels,* which later was known as *Prolegomena zur Geschichte Israels* (Berlin, 1883; English trans., Edinburgh, 1885),Vol. I, pp. 398ff., he develops the theory

more, the concept of the covenant was primarily regarded as "too legalistic." Although Pedersen in 1914 suggested the antiquity of the covenant,[7] it was Begrich[8] who focused attention upon the study of the Hebrew word *berit,* pointing to its use in the early stages of Hebrew thought. In contrast to Wellhausen's legalistic emphasis, Begrich projected the idea that the covenant represented a relationship in which the more powerful party bound the less powerful party to himself.

Beginning with E. Bickerman in 1951, serious studies have provided a comparison of covenant forms in ancient times and cultures. Mendenhall,[9] using Korosec's classic study of Hittite texts in which he offered a sixfold classification of the judicial form,[10] concluded that the same pattern prevailed in nearly all the known treaties from the latter half of the second millennium B.C. The order of the six basic elements—preamble, historical prologue, stipulations, provision of a written copy for public reading, witnesses, and innovation of curses and blessings—was so consistent that this form was recognized as characteristic of the fourteenth- and thirteenth-century B.C. treaties.

Less available currently are treaties from the first millennium B.C. Kitchen's analysis of this limited material indicates that they contain the common core of title, stipulations, witnesses, and

---

that the books of Moses from Exodus through Numbers represent a document form of postexilic times. The history of Israel was delivered and transmitted orally by priests and prophets in their religious teaching. For discussion, see W. Zimmerli, *The Law and the Prophets,* pp. 17–30.

[7] J. Pedersen, *Der Eid bei den Semiten. Studien zur Geschichte und Kultur des islamitischen Orients,* 3 (Strassburg, 1914).

[8] Joachim Begrich, "Berit. Ein Beitrag zur Erfassung einer alttestamentlichen Denkform," *Zeitschrift für die alttestamentliche Wissenschaft,* LX (1944), 1–11.

[9] G. E. Mendenhall, "Covenant Forms in Israelite Tradition," *Biblical Archaeologist,* XVII (September, 1954), 50–76.

[10] V. Korosec, *Hethitische Staatsvertrage. Ein Beitrag zu ihrer juristischen Wertung,* Leipziger rechswissenschaftliche Studien, LX (Leipzig, 1931).

curses, and some similarity in vocabulary and forms of expression.[11] These elements are obvious and essential in any covenant. The differences between the second- and first-millennium treaties are significant.The latter never place the divine witnesses between the stipulations and the curses, and do not have a historical prologue, do not have corresponding blessings for the curses, and lack consistency in order of the elements.

The obvious conclusion based on this factual comparison of suzerainty treaties of the second and first millennia B.C. is that there are similarities in the basic elements but that marked differences prevail in form and content. Evidence currently available supports the assertion made by W. F. Albright that the structure of the first-millennium treaties is quite different from the Syro-Anatolian treaties of the fourteenth and thirteenth centuries B.C., recovered primarily from the Hittite archives at Boghazköy.[12]

The striking comparison in form between the fourteenth- and thirteenth-century covenant treaties and the covenant in Exod. 20ff. has been pointedly projected by Mendenhall.[13] Other studies supporting the correspondence of the Sinai covenant with the late-second-millennium agreements are Kline,[14] Moran,[15] Harvey,[16] and Külling.[17] These data provide a reasonable basis for recognizing the account of the Sinaitic cove-

[11] Kenneth A. Kitchen, *Ancient Orient and Old Testament* (Chicago: Inter-varsity Press, 1966), pp. 94–96.

[12] Cf. William F. Albright. *From Stone Age to Christianity* (2d ed.; Garden City, N.Y.: Doubleday Anchor Books, 1957, p. 16).

[13] Cf. G. E. Mendenhall, *Law and Covenant in Israel and the Ancient Near East* (Pittsburgh, The Biblical Colloquium, 1955). See also G. von Rad, *Old Testament Theology,* Vol. I, p. 132.

[14] Cf. Kline, *op. cit.*

[15] W. L. Moran, *Biblica,* XLIII (1962), 103.

[16] J. Harvey, *op. cit.,* p. 185.

[17] S. R. Külling, *Zur Datierung der "Genesis-P-Stücke"* (*Gen. XVII*), (1964), pp. 238–39.

nant (Exod. 20–31) in its historical setting in the time of Moses. Since no factual evidence accounts for a later date in which the framework and text of Exod. 20–31 can be placed historically or dated from the standpoint of literature, the biblical setting associating this with Moses seems to be sound in the light of available evidence.

Closely related to this Sinai covenant as given in Exod. 20–31 is the renewal of the covenant under Moses after thirty-eight years of wilderness wandering as recorded in Deut. 1:1–32:47 and the Shechem covenant under Joshua (ch. 24). All three accounts have in common the six basic elements of the fourteenth- and thirteenth-century treaties.[18] Kenneth A. Kitchen has come to the conclusion that this evidence "provides tangible external ground for suggesting that considerable portions" of the books of Deuteronomy (almost the entire framework) and Joshua as well as Exodus and Leviticus (ch. 26 at least) originated in the Mosaic period. Whereas these late-second-millennium treaty patterns did not survive in surrounding civilizations —at least no evidence is currently available to this effect—the biblical books from Exodus to Joshua provide evidence of their preservation in Israelite literature and history.[19]

Thus it seems obvious that the Israelite covenant was given in the set form commonly used for treaties throughout the ancient Near East during Mosaic times. Moses used this treaty pattern in a unique way for the Israelites in expressing a divine-human relationship.

[18] For a comparison equating the six treaty elements to each of these in Exodus, Deuteronomy, and Joshua, see Kenneth A. Kitchen, *op. cit.*, pp. 96–98.

[19] Kitchen pointedly observes, "If this result obtained by a *formgeschichte* controlled by an external standard of measurement, perchance clashes either in general or in detail with certain long-cherished theories of Hebrew religious evolution or of literary criticism, then (with all due respect) so much the worse for the theories in this field" (*op. cit.*, pp. 100–1).

SIMILARITY TO TREATIES

The concept of the covenant constitutes the core of Israel's religion.[20] This is particularly true of the covenant between Israel and God as instituted at Mount Sinai and renewed under Moses and Joshua. Beyond its literary similarity in form with contemporary treaties, it rises to the sublime in expressing a unique relationship between the Israelites and their great King, the sovereign God. It transcends any merely political relationship between earthly rulers and vassal states.

Whereas the treaties with earthly rulers had to be renewed repeatedly with the same ruler or a successor in due time, Israel's covenant was with the same God throughout subsequent generations. Successive rulers might change, but the God of Israel was eternal and changeless. Consequently this treaty, or covenant, had a dimension of continuity not prevalent in contemporary treaties. Thus the blessings and curses carried implications down through successive generations. This element of continuity may account for the fact that this treaty form with all its constituent elements was so carefully preserved in Israel, whereas in other nations subsequent forms were decimated to the more simple forms available presently from the first millennium B.C.

Like other important treaties during ancient times this covenant was provided in written form. Moses wrote all the words of the agreement at Mount Sinai (Exod. 24:4). When the covenant was renewed on the Plains of Moab (Deut. 1–32), Moses provided written copies of it (Deut. 31:9), and charged the leaders with the responsibility to make God's agreement with them available in writing for future generations (Deut. 27:3–8).

[20] W. Eichrodt, *Theology of the Old Testament,* Vol. I (Philadelphia: Westminster Press, 1961).

The priests were given the solemn duty of reading the words of this covenant to each succeeding generation.

Oral communication was very important in presenting the terms of this agreement to the populace at large at periodic intervals. This oral communiqué, however, did not take the place of the written document which provided for accuracy in transmission. From the written documents the terms of the treaty were made known to each successive generation.

THE LAW WITHIN THE COVENANT

The heart of Israel's religion was not the law but the covenant. It has been increasingly recognized by Old Testament scholars that the law of God was a vital part of the covenant.[21] Since the literary work of Moses became more commonly known as "the law" in subsequent history—biblical as well as secular—the general recognition of Moses as the lawgiver has overshadowed the greater significance of Moses as the mediator of the covenant. The legal aspects—law—within the covenant are vital, but are only a subsidiary part of the covenant treaty between God and Israel. Although the laws in the ancient Near East are frequently referred to as codes, they seem to be more properly identified as law collections or legal usage. In Israel the laws, or commandments, come as stipulations within the framework of the covenant-form.[22] The fact that Israel had a collection of laws similar in numerous aspects to those of other nations should not obscure the greater significance of the relationship with God expressed in the covenant treaty.

[21] W. Zimmerli, *op. cit.,* pp. 62–63.

[22] Codes of Lipit-Ishtar, Hammurabi, and others seemed to be indirectly related to royal edicts, according to J. J. Finkelstein, *Journal of Cuneiform Studies,* XV (1961, 100–4. By comparison the books of Exodus, Deuteronomy, Joshua, and possibly Leviticus could be considered as providing commandments within the framework of the covenant form.

THE ESSENCE OF THIS RELATIONSHIP

The divine-human relationship between God and Israel uniquely distinguished the Mosaic covenant from all other contemporary treaty forms. With Moses as the mediator of this covenant the fullest account of his communication of it to Israel is preserved for us in the book of Deuteronomy.

Love was the vital core of this divine-human relationship. Love—not law—was the permeating essence in this mutual agreement between God and man as Moses expounded the meaning and significance of this treaty.[23] This idea of mutual love was to dominate the Israelites' thinking, penetrate their pattern of living, and provide the basis of their hope for the future (Deut. 5:1–11:33).

God initiated this relationship by bestowing His divine love upon the ancestors of Israel (Deut. 4:37; 10:15). The Israelites to whom Moses was speaking had not initiated this love or merited it any more than any other nation, but God through His grace and mercy had confirmed His covenantal promise to the patriarchs (Deut. 7:7–11). Significant for the Israelites was the fact that God had revealed Himself through mighty acts in redeeming them out of Egyptian bondage and sustaining them through the wilderness experiences for four decades (Deut. 1:1–4:40). This was the practical evidence of God's love for Israel.

A wholehearted unfeigned love for God by Israel—this was

[23] That the commandments as given at Mount Sinai were a subsidiary of the covenant is apparent in Moses' treatment of them in Deuteronomy. After repeating the Decalogue he elaborates primarily the First Commandment in Deut. 6–11 by emphasizing wholehearted love toward God. Moses is not so much concerned about their ability to fulfill their obligations as God's holy people as he is about their *will* to do so. In the proclamation of the law "there is no idea that Israel must be frightened by the threats which this law made" (cf. G. von Rad, *Old Testament Theology,* Vol. I [Edinburgh, 1962], p. 194).

the concern permeating Moses' appeal to the Israelites as he elaborated on the opening words of the Decalogue (Deut. chs. 5–11). The classic expression in Deut. 6:4–6 (cf. 10:12) calls for a commitment to God without any reservations, and an exclusive devotion and consecration to God alone. The Israelites were challenged to express this love to God with the entire resources of their endowed capacities. Heart, mind, and soul—all their abilities and potential strength were to be involved in exercising this love for God.

A genuine response to God's love expressed a sincere reverence and respect for Him in word as well as in the total pattern of daily living.[24] This practical acknowledgment of God in word and deed was expressed positively by the phrase "the fear of God." The individual who exhibited this respect and reverence for God in love was identified as a "God-fearing" person. Fear in the sense of "being afraid" of God arose only when the vital love relationship expressed in the first two commandments was decimated. The person whose pattern of living was threatened by the negatives had reason to be afraid of God.[25]

[24] "Love in Deuteronomy is a love that can be commanded. It is also a love intimately related to fear and reverence. Above all, it is a love which must be expressed in loyalty, in service, and in unqualified obedience to the demands of the law. For to love God is, in answer to a unique claim (6:4) to be loyal to him (11:1, 22; 30:20) to walk in his ways (10:12; 11:22; 19:9; 30:16), to keep his commandments (10:12; 11:1, 22; 19:9), to do them (11:22, 19:9), to heed them or his voice (11:30; 30:16), to serve him (10:12; 11:1, 13). It is in brief a love defined by and pledged in the covenant—a covenantal love" (cf. William L. Moran, "The Ancient Near Eastern Background of the Love of God in Deuteronomy," *Catholic Biblical Quarterly*, XXV [1963], 78).

[25] Generally "fearing God" involves reverence but in the covenantal context a disobedient vassal had reason to be afraid of having the curse sanction brought down upon him. A loyal vassal positively was fearful of offending the suzerain in violence of a trust.

"The Superior One demands from His people a constant attitude. Israel fears God in being obedient to Him. Fear of God is obedience" (cf. L. Köhler and W. Baumgartner, *Lexicon in Veteris Testamenti Libros*, Vol. I [Grand Rapids: Eerdmans, 1953], p. 56).

In the course of time legalism became a substitute for genuine devotion to God as attention was focused upon the negatives. The negative aspects or ordinances of the covenant provided a perimeter which did not affect the pattern of living normally exhibited by the individual who wholeheartedly loved God.

The positive spiritual aspect of this covenant relationship was pinpointed by Moses when he used the phrase "circumcise therefore the foreskin of your heart" (Deut. 10:16). It was not primarily the rite of circumcision—as important as that was as the sign of God's covenant—that was essential in its physical application. The heart of man which was the seat of the will must be in right relationship with God. In the same context Moses warns against stubbornness (cf. Jesus' emphasis in John 7:17). Wholehearted love for God issued in a willing conformity to the known will of God. A total absorption of God's love allowed for no other gods, for no misuse of God's name, murder, adultery, robbery, false witness, or covetousness. These became legalistic barriers only when the heart was in need of "circumcision" or the genuine reverence for God had declined. When man entertained the temptation to turn to idolatry he had reason to be afraid of God.

Love for fellow men was the natural corollary of this divine-human relationship (Deut. 10:12–22). It represented the horizontal expression of the genuine love bond between God and man. The capacity to love others had its fountainhead in an absorbing mutual love relationship with God. Genuine love for one's neighbor could only issue out of a deep-seated love for God. The Israelites had had two experiences which provided a basis for the expectation of love for their fellow men or the strangers among them—they had been the recipients of God's love (Deut. 10:15) and they had been strangers in Egypt (Deut. 10:19). Having experienced God's love in being redeemed out of Egyptain bondage they were enjoined to love their neighbors.

Social justice was the normal result when genuine love for God and for fellow men prevailed. The basis for the social gospel did not have its roots primarily in the prevailing needs but originated in God and in the nature of His being. God is not partial and does not take bribes, but executes justice for the fatherless and the widows, and loves the strangers, giving them food and clothing, therefore the person who has been the recipient of God's love is under obligation to exhibit these characteristics of God to his fellow men.[26] Moses did not outline a complete code of ethics but clearly indicated that man's total pattern of behavior should reflect the attitude of Israel's holy and just God to whom he was wholly devoted. God loved the stranger; thus anyone who claimed to be a God-fearing person should exhibit a love for his neighbor, with justice prevailing.

Having amplified the true nature of this love relationship, Moses delineates ordinances and institutions for the Israelites' pattern of living. Externally this wholehearted devotion to God found expression in cultic-ceremonial requirements which reflected the contemporary culture (Deut. 12:1–16:18). Worship, sacrifice, absolute loyalty, apostasy, nonconformity to pagan ceremonial customs, observance of feasts and seasons—all these were discussed with guidelines and instructions.

With Yahweh as God and King and as the ultimate unified authority, the Israelites were to reflect the holiness and justice of God in the political-judicial aspects of daily life (Deut.

[26] In Lev. 19 the context of "You shall love your neighbor as yourself" and other ordinances points likewise to the character of God as the basis for their ethical behavior. "You shall be holy for I the Lord your God am holy" (19:2) and "You shall love your neighbor as yourself: I am the Lord" (19:18).

16:18–21:23). Priests and later kings were to be guided in their jurisdiction by the book of the law. Prophets likewise were to project their influence in harmony with the Mosaic revelation.

The mutual relationship of citizens in the theocratic kingdom was likewise delineated by Moses (Deut. 22:1–25:29). In practice the Israelite was to show the same loving regard for his neighbor's right as for his own personal interests. Traffic in human life or disrespect for the dignity and right of others, who likewise were God's creation, had no place in the life-pattern of a people wholeheartedly devoted to God.

PERPETUATION OF THE COVENANT

Although Moses himself was the mediator through whom this covenant between God and Israel was established, he was not indispensable. With the ratification of the treaty (Deut. 27:1–30:20), the royal mediatorial representation was passed on to Joshua (Deut. 31:1–29).

Significant in the long-range perpetuation of the covenant was the provision of a written copy of this agreement here designated as "this law" (Deut. 31:9–13). This written copy was entrusted to the priests and elders who were responsible for its proclamation to the people. Every seven years this agreement was to be read publicly at the Feast of Tabernacles in the year of release (Deut. 31:10; 16:13ff.; 15:1ff.).

The explicit purpose of the reading of this agreement was that they should "hear and learn to fear" God (31:12). Neither the written copy nor the reading of it had any particular value in itself, but it provided the means to the end that the hearer might become a God-fearing person. The septennial reading of the law was an impressive reminder to the populace at large, but the basic teaching of the covenantal responsibilities was done in the home. Parents had the solemn duty to teach their children fear, reverence, and respect for God (Deut. 4:9–10). Through precept and parental example in the home, the growing child was to gain a consciousness of God's love for Israel expressed in their redemption from Egyptian bondage and their daily sustenance (Deut. 6:7–25). Consequently the home was the primary base for acquainting each successive generation with the covenant treaty between God and Israel.

The written copy of this covenant provided for accurate transmission to future generations. From this document which was placed in the custody of the priests, a written copy was to be secured by the king or ruler in Israel. He, like his fellow citizens, was to be subject to the terms of this covenant and to exemplify the fear of God (Deut. 17:18–20).

Oral transmission was the means by which the terms of this divine-human agreement were disseminated to the populace at large from this written copy at the central sanctuary. Taught in the home by parents and proclaimed publicly by the priests at the stated feasts and seasons, the laws and ordinances of this covenant treaty were made known to the entire nation.

The Israelites were assured that the Mosaic revelation which was passed on in written form would be supplemented by other prophets. Moses promised that others like him would communicate in behalf of God in subsequent generations. One criterion of a true prophet was that he would advocate a wholehearted devotion to God, agreeing with the inner spirit of the law (Deut. 13:1–5). A prophet who favored or tolerated idolatry was to be executed. Another test of a true prophet was the actual fulfillment of his prediction (Deut. 18:15–22). Consequently the Mosaic revelation became the normal standard, which was supplemented by later spokesmen for God. Basically in accord with the written revelation given through Moses, their messages modified or supplemented the Mosaic law as it was necessary for adaptation to changing times and circumstances.

IV

PROPHECY IN ISRAEL'S THEOCRACY

MOSES made provisions for both priestly and prophetic ministries in Israel. The former was established under Aaron and the Levites, while the latter was anticipated for the future. Elders were appointed during the administration of Moses and entrusted with some of the civic responsibilities.

MOSAIC PROVISIONS

Even during their Egyptian captivity, the Israelites had a representative group of men known as elders (Exod. 3:16). Moses collaborated with these men in preparation for his encounter with pharaoh. Later Moses was surrounded by seventy elders (Exod. 34:1) who shared some of the civic responsibilities with him. In anticipation of Israel's occupation of Canaan, Moses indicated that these elders should also serve as judges in apprehending murderers (Deut. 19:12), in conducting inquests (Deut. 21:2), and in settling matrimonial disputes (Deut. 22:15; 25:7). The transition from Israel's organization and encampment under Moses to a settled state in Palestine brought normal and expected changes in administration. Cities throughout the land had officials who probably came under the general classification of elders or who had responsibilities with them. Some of these are mentioned as heads of tribes (Deut.

5:23; 29:10) and as officers and judges (Josh. 8:33). Details about the number of elders for each city are not given. The city of Succoth had seventy-seven (Judg. 8:14). In later history a national body of elders is referred to in various periods (cf. I Sam. 8:4; II Sam. 5:3; I Kings 8:1, 3; 20:7; 21:8; II Kings 10:2; 21:2; 23:1; Ezek. 8:1; 14:1; 20:1).

The Levites were given responsibility for religious functions and the maintaining of worship. By virtue of sparing every first-born son in the Passover experience, God expected the oldest son in each family to be dedicated to Him. Subsequently the Levites were designated as official substitutes for the firstborn in each family (Num. 1–4) and the tithe was designated for their support (Num. 18:21–24).

With the erection of the tabernacle, the Levites were given the immediate responsibility of caring for the central sanctuary. The Levites in turn were under the direct supervision of Aaron and his sons (Num. 8:19). Aaron was the spiritual leader of Israel in matters of worship and continual ministration at the tabernacle. Under Moses he was inducted into this office (Lev. 8; Exod. 39) so that Aaron and his sons had the priestly duties of officiating at the tabernacle.

In the transition from Israel's pattern of living under Moses' leadership to that of settlement in Canaan the duties of Levites, including the priests, were somewhat adjusted and modified as supervision was decentralized. The Levites were assigned to live in forty-eight cities set aside for their use throughout Palestine (Num. 35:1ff.; Josh. 21:1ff.). In outlining the anticipated responsibilities it is quite likely that some of the duties assigned to the priests were delegated to the Levites at large. While the tabernacle with its attending priests was geographically limited to one place the ministry of the Levites was made available throughout the land.

Additional duties assigned to the Levites involving them in

various social, civic, and religious ministries were, as given in Deuteronomy: (1) to serve as judges in cases involving difficult decisions (17:8–9); (2) to regulate the supervision of lepers (24:8); (3) to guard the copies of the book of the law (17:18); and (4) to assist Moses in the covenant renewal ceremony (27:9). Some of these responsibilities pertained to various Levitical cities, while others were limited to the central sanctuary.

Through the prophetic ministry the Israelites were to maintain a continual consciousness of God's will for them. In addition to that which had been revealed through Moses and provided for them in written form, there was the need of knowing God's will as it pertained to the current developments in each generation. Through the Urim and Thummim, which were kept in the high priest's breastplate (Exod. 28:30; Lev. 8:8), the priest was endowed with the ability to declare the will of God. Significantly, this provision is made with the ordination of Joshua to leadership (Num. 27:18–23). Whereas this seemed to be the means of providing a knowledge of God's will to those who inquired, the ministry of a prophet as outlined by Moses was that of positive and active proclamation of His will. In two passages Moses assures the Israelites that men will come as God's representatives to make known His messages as needed. In the course of Israel's history, the ministry of men who were especially commissioned to speak God's messages apparently replaced the use of the Urim and Thummim by the priests.

The priests were the custodians of the law. To them was committed the written copy of the agreement between God and His people Israel. It was their responsibility to make the content of this written copy available to the people as well as the leaders throughout subsequent generations.

Parents were under obligation to teach their children about their relationship with God. The home was the basic institution in which the Israelites were to maintain this vital relationship with God and contagiously impart it to each succeeding generation. In the home the growing children were continually made conscious of God by numerous external means as outlined in Deut. 4–6. Parents were admonished to remind the next generation of God's mighty acts in redeeming them out of Egypt. This great miracle of redemption they should never forget as a nation. The core and essence of parental teaching was not merely an intellectual knowledge and understanding of the law or primarily orthodox doctrine but was, rather, a proper conception of knowledge and reverence for God. The "fear of God" so frequently referred to throughout the Bible is not a matter of "being afraid of God" but a practical understanding that the God who had redeemed Israel was a God of love and that His mercy would be extended everlastingly to those who loved and revered Him. This concept of God could be effectively taught to children only by precept and example. As parents expressed this wholehearted commitment and love toward God in their daily lives, the children became acquainted with a pattern of living in which God was continually and consistently recognized. The septennial public reading of the covenant requirements aided in the oral dissemination of the law to the entire nation.

The leaders of Israel were also expected to conform to the law of Moses. Their responsibility was to set an example of faithfully observing the requirements revealed through Moses and preserved in written form. Whether the leader was a military general, a judge, a priest, a prophet, or a king, it was his first duty to acknowledge the fact that he was a member of God's covenant nation. He was expected to exemplify a wholehearted commitment to God. Although copies of the law may have been rare and expensive at that time, Moses made provision so that a ruler in Israel was to be provided by the priests with a personal copy. Kingship in Israel was unique in that the king did not have sole authority, but like his people was to be obedient to the law.

The prophetic function of reminding the Israelites in post-Mosaic times of the mutual responsibilities between God and Israel is exemplified in subsequent history. Leaders vary in their particular responsibility depending upon the circumstances and needs in their generation. In the course of Israel's transition from a theocracy to a kingship this prophetic function becomes more essential.

ERA OF CONQUEST

Joshua was divinely commissioned to lead the Israelites in the conquest and occupation of Canaan. Although he was primarily a military leader, for which he was qualified by experience under Moses (Exod. 17), his success was conditioned on conformity to the requirements prescribed by Moses (Josh. 1:1–9). It was Joshua, however, and not the priests, who was in command as they entered Canaan. From the very beginning Joshua was concerned with his responsibility to comply with the law of Moses. Before the Israelites conquered Jericho they observed the Passover, vividly reminding them of their deliverance from Egypt. The rite of circumsion was administered under Joshua's direction, imparting to the new generation the physical sign of the covenant. After the conquest of Ai, Joshua exposed the Israelites to the reading of the law as they were encamped between the mountains of Ebal and Gerizim (Josh. 8:30–35). Before his death he expressed a genuine concern that they should remain faithful in their devotion to God. In his appeal he realized that each succeeding generation needed to renew its relationship with God.

Another prophetic function of Joshua was that of prediction. Encamped before the river Jordan he announced that God would perform mighty acts or wonders before the Israelites (Josh.

3:5). In the miraculous provision for the passage of Israel through the river, Joshua was publicly confirmed as the divinely appointed leader of Israel. Thus God provided the prophetic confirmation identifying Joshua as a true spokesman for Him, as Moses had indicated in Deut. 18:22.

Another prediction given through Joshua was related to the initial victory of the Israelites in Canaan. Divine assurance of the fall of Jericho was provided in God's message through Joshua before the Israelites marched around the city (Josh. 6:2ff.). In this way Joshua was divinely confirmed as military leader for the Israelites.

Joshua's vital concern about Israel's relationship with God is expressed in the renewal of the covenant before his death (ch. 24). In the conquest and occupation of Canaan, the Israelites had been victorious to the extent of their obedience. In the possession of the land they were assured of benefits and blessings as they maintained an attitude of obedience and faithfulness to the commandments of Jehovah, their Great King.

Six basic elements are clearly stated in this renewal treaty.[1] The stipulations are adapted to a dialogue form as Joshua emphasizes their obligations.[2] Since the stipulations of Deuteronomy are still in effect there is no needless repetition in this ceremony, but Joshua does single out the Israelites' basic responsibility in the words: "Fear Jehovah, and serve him in sincerity and truth" (24:14). This "fearing God" in the Deuteronomic covenant meant nothing less than walking in God's ways, loving and serving Him with heart and soul, keeping

[1] The six parts are as follows: Preamble, 24:2; Prologue, 23:3–14; Stipulations, 24:14–19; Curses and blessings, 24:20; Witnesses, 24:22; Perpetuation, 24:25–28. Dennis J. McCarthy, *Treaty and Covenant* (Rome: Pontifical Biblical Institute, 1963), pp. 145–48, divides this covenant into an extremely rigid form of eleven parts.

[2] Cf. Charles H. Giblin, "Structural Patterns in Joshua 24:1–25," *Catholic Biblical Quarterly*, XXVI (1964), 51.

His commandments and statutes (Deut. 10:12–13, 20; 28:58).[3]

In this dialogue Joshua repeatedly appeals to the Israelites to maintain a vital relationship with God which will be expressed in their daily pattern of living as they serve God in doing that which He requires of them. The details were known to them through the Mosaic revelation.

PERIOD OF THE JUDGES

The moral and spiritual breakdown came in the post-Joshua era. The newer generations, not having witnessed the mighty acts of God which had been manifested through Joshua, turned to idolatry. This apostasy was a breaking of the first commandment and indicated an obvious neglect of that wholehearted love and commitment that was so essential in their relationship with God. So prevalent was the apostasy that God's judgment was exercised through invading nations. These oppressions were designed to make the Israelites conscious of their apostasy (Judg. 2:20–23). Intermarriage with those who were not devoted to God resulted in disintegration of the home. Instead of being taught by their parents to revere and love God, the children were led astray into idolatry. The severity of these oppressions repeatedly stimulated repentance and ultimately brought relief as God responded to their appeals for mercy.

God's communication to the Israelites during the era of the judges came through mighty acts as well as through the prophetic word. Relatively little detail is given in the biblical account, but the basic fact throughout is that these military leaders were motivated to action by divine initiative. Concerning some of these men it is recorded that the spirit of the Lord came upon them (Judg. 3:10; 11:20; 13:25). For others such as Gideon and

[3] Cf. Ludwig Köhler, *Old Testament Theology* (Philadelphia: The Westminster Press, 1957), pp. 55–56.

Samson extensive details are given concerning their preparation for delivering the Israelites from their oppressors. Although they had the law of Moses they did not obey it. Perhaps the question raised by Gideon was repeatedly asked in succeeding generations, ". . . and where be all the miracles which our fathers told us of . . . ?" (Judg. 6:13). By raising up these judges God made Himself known to successive generations as they witnessed and experienced deliverance through miracles.

Divine communication came also through theophanies. Angelic messengers appeared in connection with Gideon's call and Samson's birth. Through these God made known His will regarding the particular situation in response to Israel's cry for divine aid. Messages of prediction with the assurance of divine deliverance from oppressing nations were given in both instances (Judg. 6:14 and 13:5).

The words "prophet" and "prophetess" appear once each in the book of Judges. Little is known about Deborah beyond the fact that she was recognized by the Israelites for an effective ministry in rendering judgment. She spoke as God's messenger to Barak, indicating that through him divine deliverance from Canaanite oppression was in the offing. The predictive element in her message was the promise that the superior forces of Sisera would be defeated (Judg. 4:7, 14). This organic prediction was fulfilled in divinely timed weather conditions that gave Barak the advantage over the Canaanites (Judg. 5:4, 20). The secondary prediction involving the death of Sisera by Jael, instead of by soldiers on the field of battle, made it apparent that God was in control and aided His people.

An unnamed prophet is briefly noted in the days of Gideon (Judg. 6:7–10). He came as God's messenger during the Midianite oppression when the Israelites were appealing for divine aid. His message was brief and to the point. They had not obeyed God who had delivered them out of Egypt and enabled them to occupy Canaan but had turned to idols. Instead of revering God they had revered idols.

How extensively the priests and elders disseminated the knowledge of the written law during the era of the judges is not indicated. It is apparent, however, that Jephthah as well as the parents of Samson reflect rather detailed acquaintance with Israel's history and their sacrifices as recorded in the Pentateuch (Judg. 11; 13). The only reference to the central sanctuary is in Judg. 18:1, indicating that the tabernacle was located at Shiloh. The last five chapters in Judges do reflect the religious and moral laxity prevalent throughout the nation.

The low ebb of Israel's religion is realistically exemplified in the life of Eli, who had the responsibility of serving as both judge and priest at Shiloh. Eli's failure to teach his sons, Hophni and Phinehas, the essence of Israel's religion was apparent in their lack of respect and love for God and for their fellow Israelites. As priests they had no regard for God ("they knew not the Lord," I Sam. 2:12). Instead of exemplifying reverence for God and teaching the requirements as projected in the Mosaic revelation these sons took advantage of the Israelites who brought their sacrifices to the tabernacle in Shiloh. In addition Hophni and Phinehas were guilty of immoral behavior with the women who assembled at the tabernacle (I Sam. 2:12–17, 22–25).

Israel's religion declined to such a naturalistic conception of God that the Israelites prevailed upon the sons of Eli to bring the Ark of the covenant, which symbolized God's presence, into the battlefield (I Sam. 4:1–22). Evidenced by their jubilant reaction was the assumption of the people that God was among them to defeat the Philistines. When news came that his sons had been killed and the Ark of God had been taken by the Philistines, Eli, still sensitive to the seriousness of the situation, died of shock.

THE PROPHET SAMUEL

With apostasy prevailing at Shiloh, God revealed himself through God-fearing laity. Hannah expressed her concern through prayer and subsequently became the mother of a son through whom the consciousness of God was restored to Israel. Concurrently, during this period when Samuel was born and reared in the tabernacle environment, an unnamed man of God came to deliver a message of judgment to Eli. Speaking for God, he warned Eli that he had failed to honor God in his lack of disciplining his sons. This prophet predicted judgment in the death of Eli's sons and the ultimate removal of his family from the priesthood in Israel (I Sam. 2:27–36). The reminder by this man of God that Eli's family had been chosen to serve when Israel was delivered from Egypt reflects a knowledge of the Pentateuchal laws and narratives. Although the organic prediction of the removal of Eli's family from the priesthood did not occur for several generations, the incidental prophecy about the death of Eli's sons was fulfilled in his lifetime.

God's revelation was further enlarged through Samuel in both positive and negative aspects. Samuel's call to be a prophet provided constructive leadership while the impending judgment upon the house of Eli was reaffirmed. Samuel's first message was a solemn word of rebuke and judgment for the national leader of Israel who had failed in his parental and priestly responsibilities. Eli's iniquity was beyond purging by sacrifice or offering (I Sam. 3:11–14).

With Eli's death, Samuel emerged as the national leader of Israel. His primary concern was for the Israelites to renew their spiritual relationship with God. He reminded them of the vital truth that they had broken the first commandment in turning to idolatry (I Sam. 7:3). He predicted that God would give them victory over the Philistines if they would turn to Him in repentance. After Samuel officiated in sacrifice and prayed for his people, God's revelation to Israel was manifested in His mighty acts on their behalf. The Philistines were defeated through divine intervention (I Sam. 7:10). By emphasizing the importance of Israel's relationship with God as outlined in the written body of revelation that had been given through Moses, the prophet Samuel led Israel back into a pattern of living in which they enjoyed God's favor and blessing.

Samuel was nationally recognized as a judge, a priest, and a prophet. Making his circuit annually throughout Israel, he served effectively as judge. In his priestly function he officiated at sacrifices at such cities as Ramah, Mizpah, Bethlehem, Gilgal, and other places. As a prophet he was known as the man of God (I Sam. 9:6–7, 10) and recognized throughout the land from Dan to Beersheba (I Sam. 3:19–21). When Samuel began to delegate his responsibilities, the Israelites requested a king. Consequently Samuel had a significant influence in Israel as they changed from theocracy to kingship.

Although Samuel advised the Israelites against having a king, it was divinely revealed to him that he should comply with their request. Subsequently he anointed Saul and later David as kings in Israel.

The uniqueness of Israel's relationship with God was to be maintained even in the transition to kingship. God's revelation to Samuel was explicit. Saul was anointed "prince over my people Israel" (I Sam. 9:16; 10:1). Consequently a king was under obligation to be obedient to God. As king he had stewardship responsibilities to rule over God's people with a fixed accountability to God. He, as well as the people, was subject to the law of God (Deut. 17:14–20).

Through Samuel the prophet, the conditions of success were outlined for Saul. Even though the Israelites belittled him, Saul was assured that the spirit of God would come upon him.

Previously men like Gideon, Jephthah, and Samson had been endued for the purpose of giving Israel relief from oppressing enemies. Saul experienced a manifestation of God's spirit even before he was publicly anointed (I Sam. 10). Samuel in his role as prophet assured Saul and his people that if they would wholeheartedly love and serve God (I Sam. 12), they would be assured of His presence among them. Subsequently the spirit of God came upon Saul to effect a victory over the Ammonites. Later, when Saul disobeyed, warnings came repeatedly through Samuel. Yielding to impatience Saul acted foolishly in officiating at a sacrifice, which was a priestly duty (I Sam. 13). Instead of executing the assignment to punish the Amalekites, Saul substituted sacrifice for obedience and thus forfeited the kingdom.

Conditions worsened as Saul, in his attitude of defiance of the divinely revealed will of God as known to him through the Mosaic law and through Samuel, continued to rule. Concurrently God's message had come to Samuel that David had been chosen to be captain over God's inheritance, the people of Israel (I Sam. 13:14). When Samuel died, all the Israelites gathered to lament the death of this great prophet of the Lord (I Sam. 25:1).

THE DAVIDIC ERA

The life of David represents the epitome of God's revelation through one man who served as both prophet and king in Israel. In spite of his failures and shortcomings, David was genuinely and realistically concerned about his relationship with God. The Mosaic-theocratic rule in Israel found expression in David's reign and was never equaled after his death. Consequently the reign of David was repeatedly the point of reference in the prophetic messages as the ideal of the kingdom of Israel.

Throughout his life, David was sensitive in maintaining an

attitude of dependence upon God and a wholehearted commitment to God as outlined in the Mosaic revelation. In his early years he learned to depend upon God for care and protection when he was responsible for his father's flocks (I Sam. 17:37). Concern for God's honor motivated David to trust Him to aid him in challenging Goliath (I Sam. 17:26). He was confident that through God's power manifested in this victory, the knowledge of God would be widely evident (I Sam. 17:46). Throughout the period when Saul sought his life, David was conscious of God's protection (Ps. 18, and others). Repeatedly he refused to kill the Lord's anointed (I Sam. 24:6).

When David was recognized as king of all Israel he demonstrated a genuine concern for public acknowledgment of God by making Jerusalem the center of worship. This ultimately led to plans to build a temple, but David himself was not permitted to execute this project. By organizing the priests and Levites, by purchasing a site for the temple, by making commercial arrangements with Hiram, the king of Tyre, and by writing numerous psalms for worship, David anticipated a national recognition and worship of God such as Israel had never before experienced as a powerful nation.

David was a brilliant militarist. Successfully he gained the military advantage over the surrounding nations and established the supremacy of Israel in the heart of the Fertile Crescent. These achievements were acknowledged by David as a manifestation of God's power. In Ps. 18 and II Sam. 22, he expresses his gratitude to God for His mighty acts in behalf of Israel. In this manner God's power was displayed in behalf of His covenant people through David, who was confirmed as captain of God's inheritance.

David maintained an attitude of compliance with the basic terms of Israel's covenant relationship with God as revealed through Moses. Idolatry, which was Israel's besetting sin during the era of the judges, is hardly mentioned in association with David's reign as it is portrayed in the books of II Samuel and I Chronicles. At the close of his reign, David instructed Solomon to obey the law of Moses, calling to his attention the implications of obedience and disobedience (I Kings 2:3). With a similar emphasis, David charged the princes, the leaders, and the nation as a whole to give heed to God and His requirements (I Chron. 28:8). Love and devotion to God expressed in obedience was the key to Israel's enjoyment of God's continued blessing.

The prophetic revelation in Davidic times was supplemental to that which had been given previously. The prophets most active in association with David were Nathan and Gad. The former at first concurred with David in his plan to build the temple, but subsequent to God's revelation to him Nathan advised David to the contrary. The divine promise given through Nathan at this time assured David, however, that his throne would be established eternally. When David ignored God temporarily in taking Bathsheba as his wife at the expenditure of Uriah's life, it was Nathan the prophet who rebuked the king of Israel for his great sin.

The prophet Gad was another spokesman for God who ministered to King David in time of crisis. Apparently David was guilty of pride in the census that he conducted in spite of Joab's objections, and consequently judgment came upon Israel. Through Gad the divine message was made known to David and ultimately through this experience the site of the temple was purchased and fixed.

The vital relationship that David normally had with God is extensively and beautifully reflected in the psalms. Repeatedly he expresses his love and wholehearted devotion to God. Approximately seventy-five psalms are associated with David. In the penitential psalms, such as Ps. 32 and Ps. 51, David freely speaks of his deep sense of guilt and sinfulness as well as of his consciousness of God's abounding mercy in the personal forgiveness of his sin.[4] In Psalms 21, 37, and others, David as king of Israel expresses his confidence in God in whom is the source of blessing for his people. In Psalm 19 and similar passages he conveys his recognition of God's revelation in nature.

In numerous psalms the messianic hopes are considerably enlarged through David, who had been assured through Nathan that his throne would be established forever. In Psalm 22 David portrays the suffering and death of the Messiah as well as the universal extension of God's kingdom. The hope of the resurrection is expressed in Psalm 16 and others. In the New Testament, Christ and the apostles acknowledge David as a prophet who spoke of future events such as the death and resurrection which were fulfilled in Jesus Christ, whom David in his psalms already had acknowledged as his Lord. The establishment of the universal kingdom as hopefully expressed by David was recognized in New Testament times as rightfully belonging to the future developments.

Through Solomon, God's revelation continued. He began his reign displaying the wisdom divinely imparted in response to his prayer, experienced the manifestation of God's presence as the

[4] David's experience as expressed in these two psalms against the background of II Sam. 11–12 offers a realistic insight into personal religion in Old Testament times. Confession of sin was as essential to a vital relationship with God as it was later in New Testament times. When David prays "create in me a clean heart" he is as conscious of a supernatural work in his life as the New Testament writers are when they speak of "being born again," "a new creature in Christ," a "new life," and similar expressions. David's hope for forgiveness was not primarily vested in the sacrifices per se but in the attitude expressed in a "broken and contrite heart," or a "broken spirit." The external or legalistic approach could never be a substitute for a vital personal relationship with God.

The divine guidance David identifies in Ps. 32:8 seems to have been as genuine in his life as that which is identified with the Holy Spirit in the fuller revelation in the New Testament.

divine glory filled the temple at the time of its dedication, and received the subsequent acclaim of surrounding nations. In the course of time, however, Solomon became lax in his relationship with God, ignored the Mosaic restrictions as given in Deut. 17, and tolerated idolatry. Consequently, rival leaders rose to influence and power so that after Solomon's death the great Israelite kingdom was divided (I Kings 11). Though Solomon was acclaimed as the wisest man in history, he was usually ignored by the prophets, since he failed in maintaining a vital relationship with God.

In subsequent periods the kingdom of David is proclaimed as the ideal kingdom. Prophet after prophet used David and his kingdom as the point of reference when the hopes of restoration in the universal kingdom were outlined. The prevalence of the knowledge of God throughout David's kingdom marked a decided advance and realistic supplement to the Mosaic revelation. As king and prophet, David had a vivid perspective of the Messiah who would come as one of his descendants to establish a universal kingdom.

V

PROPHETS TEMPER APOSTASY

CRUCIAL in the history of Israel's religion was the apostasy of Solomon (I Kings 11:9–13). Although God had revealed himself twice to Solomon, the king of Israel failed positively in not maintaining a wholehearted commitment to God and negatively in turning to idolatry. Consequently, when Solomon died the extensive kingdom which he had inherited from David was divided (II Kings 11–12). The Davidic dynasty was immediately confined to an area of approximately 3,000 to 3,500 square miles between the Dead Sea and the Mediterranean Sea bounded by the Sinaitic desert on the south and, on the north, by the Northern Kingdom, which had an area almost three times as large. Territories beyond these borders formerly included under David declared their independence. In subsequent periods repeated threats challenged the continuation of the Davidic line of rulers in the small kingdom of Judah often designated as the Southern Kingdom.

When kings in the Northern Kingdom as well as in the Southern Kingdom turned to idolatry, the prophets faced the hazardous responsibility of keeping the Israelites conscious of their relationship with God as His covenant people. Consequently they frequently became involved in state affairs, especially when their God-given messages related to national and international problems. They had the responsibility of encouraging God's people—kings as well as laity—to place their hope and confidence in God rather than in their own resources of wisdom such as foreign alliances. Following Moses' example, they exhorted the people to acknowledge God in their pattern of living. Their teaching ministry was ancillary to the law of Moses, supplementing it with that which was revealed through them concerning the particular circumstances at that time. Keenly conscious of the coming judgment upon apostate Israel, the prophets provided further light on the restoration and the realization of God's purpose in using Israel as a witness to the heathen nations.

Numerous prophets were active in Israel whose messages are but briefly noted in the historical books. Better known are those prophets whose names have been attached to their messages in the Old Testament canon. Each prophet was vitally concerned with the man-God relationship. Idolatry, which seemed to be the besetting sin, provided external evidence that the people had departed from their wholehearted devotion and love for God. The social evils of the time reflected their lack of love for their fellow men.

PROPHETS COUNSEL NEW LEADERS

The prophet Ahijah explicitly exposed the reasons for the disintegration of the Davidic kingdom when he promised Jeroboam that he would be ruler of the Northern Kingdom (I Kings 11:26–40). Solomon's failure to maintain a God-fearing attitude as David had done precipitated divine judgment. For David's sake the throne would be preserved on a limited basis. Jeroboam, however, was assured that his throne would be established on the condition of his obedience. Idolatry on his part would result in his forfeiting the kingdom. Near the close of his reign, Jeroboam sent his wife to Ahijah at Shiloh for advice (I Kings 14:1–20). The prophet predicted the death of Jeroboam's sick son. In addition came the warning that Jeroboam's dynasty would be terminated because of his idolatry and his failure to keep the law.

Another prophet warned Jeroboam at the beginning of his reign about idolatry. This prophet is merely identified as a man of God from Judah (I Kings 13).[1] Jeroboam disregarded the warnings about adhering to the law, erected altars, appointed priests to his liking, and set before Israel the example of idolatry. When the man of God rebuked Jeroboam for officiating at the altar in Bethel, the king ordered the arrest of the prophet. Two miracles were performed confirming this prophet as God's messenger. Jeroboam's arm was paralyzed and restored, and the altar was rent in accordance with the prophet's word. The latter should have provided undeniable evidence to the king as well as to his people that God was currently revealing Himself, making His will known through this prophet.[2] In spite of this warning, Jeroboam persisted in his idolatrous ways, which precipitated God's judgment upon himself and his kingdom.

Shemaiah was the prophet in Judah at the crucial time when the Solomonic kingdom was partitioned. When Rehoboam planned to subdue the northern rebellion under Jeroboam by force, Shemaiah conveyed God's message warning the king not to interfere (I Kings 12:20–24). Rehoboam was sensitive to the prophet's message as he began his reign. His adherence to the

[1] Josephus identifies this prophet from Judah as Jadon. In II Chron. 9:29, Jedo or Jedai is mentioned as a source for the history of Solomon. This may be the Jadon of Josephus. (*Antiquities,* VIII, 8.)

[2] Even prophets, though they were spokesmen for God, were under obligation to obey God. This is clearly illustrated in I Kings 13 where this man of God from Judah was killed en route home because he had accepted the invitation from the resident prophet in Bethel. Initially he was forbidden to accept any hospitality while on this mission.

law may have been stimulated by the Levites who were dismissed from priestly service by Jeroboam and in turn migrated in large numbers to the kingdom of Judah. When Rehoboam was established as king, he and his people became unfaithful in their devotion to God as prescribed in the law. Shemaiah once more had a message interpreting the current development in which Shishak was threatening Jerusalem as an act of God. In response to their repentance Rehoboam and the leaders were assured that Shishak's invasion would be limited and would not be final as far as Jerusalem was concerned (II Chron. 11–12).

REVERSING RELIGIOUS TRENDS

Azariah, the son of Oded, was empowered by the Spirit of God to bring a message of encouragement during an era when Asa took the initiative in a reform movement. Under Rehoboam and Abijah idol worship prevailed throughout the land of Judah, but Asa made extensive reforms in removing idolatry even to the point of demoting his mother, Maacah, from being queen (I Kings 15:11–13). Even though the priests converged *en masse* from all Palestine and took up residence in Judah in the days of Rehoboam and were used by King Abijah in his war against Jeroboam (II Chron. 13), the first two decades following Solomon's death were characterized by a dearth of teaching priests who were concerned about the law (II Chron. 15:3). When Asa, king of Judah, expressed a concern to seek after God and then experienced God's act of deliverance in victory over the Ethiopians, the prophet Azariah (Oded) encouraged Asa in his reformation. By the fifteenth year of his reign, Asa's revival in Judah drew not only the citizens of Judah but also those of the northern tribes to Jerusalem. This religious interest in participating in the revival in Jerusalem by the citizens of the Northern Kingdom led to the fortification of Ramah by King Baasha to prevent such pilgrimages.[3]

The international crisis precipitated by this development provided the occasion for the prophet Hanani to deliver God's message of rebuke to Asa, king of Judah. Asa solved the problem of Baasha's aggression by using temple treasures to bribe Benhadad, king of Syria, into an alliance. When the latter attacked cities near Israel's northern border, Baasha abandoned the Ramah project, moving his armies north. Consequently Asa occupied Ramah to his own advantage. Hanani's criticism pertained to the man-God relationship which represented the core of the Mosaic covenant. Asa had lapsed in his wholehearted devotion to God and trusted in his own wisdom to solve this problem. He had experienced God's revelation in a mighty act of deliverance when he was faced by a superior force. Consequently he had experiential evidence for believing that God would have helped him in this crisis. Asa had acted foolishly by relying on his own wisdom. Reacting adversely to this rebuke the king imprisoned Hanani, causing the prophet to suffer for delivering God's message. Later during his reign, Asa himself was subjected to physical suffering but even in this he did not return to an attitude of seeking after God. Hanani may be one of the prophets Hosea (8:9) refers to as being hated in the house of his God.

Jehu, the son of Hanani, was God's spokesman to announce judgment upon the dynasty of Baasha. Although he had been enabled to destroy the royal family of Jeroboam in judgment for their idolatrous ways, Baasha himself was guilty of idolatry.

[3] The thirty-sixth year in II Chron. 16:1 is best explained as the thirty-sixth year of the Southern Kingdom since Solomon's death, making this actually the sixteenth year of Asa (cf. E. R. Thiele, *The Mysterious Numbers of the Hebrew Kings* [Chicago: University of Chicago Press, 1951], pp. 57–60).

Divine judgment would come in a similar manner on the family of Baasha repeatedly throughout his reign (I Kings 16:1–8).

BAALISM CHALLENGED

Elijah came with God's message during a period of unprecedented political power and national idolatry in the Northern Kingdom. Omri built Samaria as Israel's capital and successfully promoted a policy of friendship with surrounding nations so that his kingdom was stronger than it had been since its beginning in 931 under Jeroboam. The Israelite-Phoenician alliance was sealed by the marriage of Omri's son, Ahab, to Jezebel, the daughter of Ethbaal, king of Tyre. As a result idolatry was promoted to excess as Ahab and Jezebel made Baal worship the official religion of Israel. In Samaria a temple was erected to Baal. Even though Ahab provoked more divine displeasure than had any king before him (I Kings 16:30–33), God revealed Himself more extensively in miracles and specific guidance through Elijah and Elisha than the Israelites had experienced since the time of Solomon.

Boldly Elijah faced Ahab when Jezebel was silencing the prophets of the Lord throughout the land (I Kings 18:4 and 13). Elijah was concerned about the man-God relationship. The warning about the lack of rain conditioned Ahab and the people for the public assembly on Mount Carmel. Elijah's public prayer for a miraculous ignition of the sacrifice in order that the Israelites might know that the Lord God was the God of the patriarchs was answered (I Kings 18:36).[4] Other predictions concerning the drought and subsequent rain were likewise fulfilled in accordance with Elijah's word. Consequently Elijah

[4] Although Elijah's call is not recorded, his actions and this request for public confirmation indicate that he had a divine call to the prophetic ministry.

was established as a prophet in Israel by miracles even as Moses had been during the exodus.

Elijah had his times of discouragement. Threatened by Jezebel he fled southward where he experienced an angelic revelation at Beersheba, which strengthened him. At Mount Horeb in another divine revelation he received specific instructions to continue as God's servant (I Kings 19:9–18). When Elijah expressed concern about Israel's broken relationship with God, lamented the fact that the altars of God had been wrecked, and grieved over the martyred prophets, he was assured that there still were 7,000 God-fearing people who had not capitulated to idolatry. Elijah was encouraged by the predictions given relative to his continued service as a prophet, being made conscious anew of the fact that God controls the affairs of nations even as had been exemplified in Israel's history since Mosaic times. Included in his assignment were the replacements of the ruling families in both Israel and Syria. Elijah was also assured of the termination of the Baal-devoted dynasty which he was opposing. The prophetic ministry, on the other hand, would continue through his successor, Elisha. In this way Baalism would be countered by a threefold thrust in the rise of a strong aggressive king, Hazael, in Syria; in Jehu taking control in Israel; and in Elisha's supporting and continuing ministry. Almost immediately Elisha joined Elijah. Through the former both Hazael and Jehu were informed of their royal responsibilities.

Unnamed prophets were active during Ahab's reign. In I Kings 20 they were identified as "a prophet" in verse 20, as "a man of God" in verse 28, and as "a certain man of the sons of the prophets" in verse 35. Grappling with the problems of warfare Ahab called the Israelite elders together for counsel. At this crucial moment an unnamed prophet came with God's message expressing divine concern for the man-God relationship. This prophet promised God's manifestation in mighty acts of deliverance for the purpose that "thou shalt know that I am the Lord" (v. 13). A second victory over the Syrians was given to Ahab subsequently—again with a divinely revealed interpretation so that "ye shall know that I am the Lord" (v. 28). Ahab, however, did not acknowledge these prophets to the extent of asking their advice in time of victory, but made a covenant with Benhadad, king of Syria. Consequently Ahab was warned that he as king as well as his nation would suffer the consequences. Instead of turning to God in repentance, Ahab returned to Samaria embittered and angry (vv. 42–43).

Elijah had one more encounter with Ahab (I Kings 21). After Ahab and Jezebel disregarded the law of inheritance as given in the Mosaic law and ignored justice and righteousness in the execution of Naboth, Elijah was commissioned to deliver another message from God to Ahab. The king of Israel was solemnly warned by the prophet that, for his guilt in the stoning of Naboth and his illegal possession of the vineyard, his life would be terminated in such a manner that dogs would lick his blood and that his dynasty would be exterminated. When Ahab temporarily repented, the verdict concerning the extermination of his family was postponed to the next generation.

The final encounter between Ahab and true prophets is vividly portrayed in I Kings 22. Ahab and Jehoshaphat, whose alliance was sealed by the marriage of Jehoram and Athaliah, were about to recapture Ramoth in Gilead from Syrian control. As Jehoshaphat agreed to aid Ahab in this venture, he requested that they should ascertain the "word of the Lord" (v. 5). When 400 prophets of Ahab unanimously avowed that "the Lord shall deliver it into the hand of the king," Jehoshaphat asked for "a prophet of the Lord," implying that Ahab's prophets were false. When Ahab agreed to call Micaiah, the prophets of Ahab led by Zedekiah unanimously continued their assurance that this military engagement would be successful. Micaiah appeared before the kings and this assembly of prophets with the condition that he would deliver God's message. When Micaiah concurred with the advice given by the prophets, Ahab recognized his mockery and demanded that he should declare to him God's word. In response Micaiah clearly predicted the death of Ahab and the defeat of Israel. For this Micaiah was imprisoned by Ahab with the order that he not be released until Ahab returned from battle.

Having full knowledge of this divinely revealed message Ahab resorted to his own wisdom. Hoping to avoid identification he disguised himself as he went into battle. Micaiah's prediction, however, was fulfilled when a stray arrow wounded Ahab in battle. Elijah's prediction was likewise fulfilled—the dogs licked the blood of Ahab after he returned to Samaria in his chariot fatally wounded.

PIETY AND TOLERANCE

The Southern Kingdom during the time of Ahab provides a contrast to idolatrous Israel. The man-God relationship was nationally established and maintained through Jehoshaphat (II Chron. 17–20). As king he set the example of seeking after God and sent princes, priests, and Levites throughout the land to instruct the people in the Mosaic law. He was concerned about removing idolatry, although some of the high places were still retained in certain areas. In times of national emergency Jehoshaphat himself stood before his people humbly confessing his dependence upon God and advising his people to believe God's prophets. Personally he reflected considerable knowledge of Israel's history and law in addressing his people. In appointing judges throughout the kingdom, Jehoshaphat reminded them of the essence of the Mosaic revelation which indicated that they should fear or revere God (II Chron. 19:7) and that they should administer their duties as judges according to the principles of justice prescribed in the law. Cases that could not be solved in the local cities could be brought to Jerusalem where elders, priests, and Levites officiated.

For his ungodly alliances Jehoshaphat was severely rebuked. Returning from participation in Ahab's final battle with the Syrians in which his life was providentially spared, Jehoshaphat was met by the prophet Jehu, the son of Hanani. The king of Judah was solemnly rebuked for helping the ungodly and loving those who hate the Lord (II Chron. 19:1–2). Love for man could only be expressed in the context of a wholehearted love and devotion for God.

Eliezer was another prophet who rebuked Jehoshaphat for his alliance with the wicked Omride dynasty (II Chron. 20:35–37). The joint naval venture of Jehoshaphat and Ahaziah failed when their ships were wrecked as had been predicted by this prophet of the Lord.

Elisha also made Jehoshaphat conscious of his association with wicked kings (II Kings 3) when he joined Joram, the son of Ahab, and the king of Edom in war against Mesha, the king of Moab. In desperation when their water supply failed, these kings appealed to Elisha who happened to be in the Israelite camp. It was Jehoshaphat's request for a prophet through whom inquiry of God could be made that revealed Elisha's presence. Since the king of Israel was in command of this military expedition, Elisha retorted that Joram should consult the prophets of Ahab and Jezebel. Resigned to doom unless divine aid was forthcoming Joram pleaded with Elisha. The prophet Elisha boldly replied that he would abandon them to their fate if it were not for his regard for Jehoshaphat. Then Elisha assured them of the Lord's provision of an adequate water supply and also of a victory over Moab.

ELISHA'S EXTENDED MINISTRY

The prophetic ministry of Elisha, in which God's mighty acts and messages were made known to Israel in a more extensive manner than through Elijah, began in the days of Ahab and continued for approximately four decades under the dynasty of Jehu. The last recorded confrontation between Elijah and the Omride rulers occurred when Ahaziah, the son of Ahab, sent messengers to Baalzebub, the god of Ekron (II Kings 1). Sent by divine command, Elijah stopped the messengers, predicted that Ahaziah would not recover, and finally appeared in person before the king announcing God's judgment. The fulfillment of this prediction brought Joram, another son of Ahab, to the throne in Israel.

Elisha was very active during the twelve years of Joram's reign, which ended in judgment as the Omride dynasty, including Jezebel and many Baal zealots, was exterminated. Elisha's fame extended throughout Israel and beyond as he continued teaching in the schools of the prophets founded by Elijah. Through miraculous aid he provided for numerous people in their needs. For a widow he multiplied her oil to redeem her sons from possible enslavement, to the Shunammite woman's son he restored life, and for the sons of the prophets he provided food (II Kings 4). Through Elisha's instructions Naaman, the Syrian captain, secured healing from his leprosy. When one of the students lost his axhead Elisha miraculously recovered it.

Elisha had direct contact with King Joram on numerous occasions. In the war against Moab he boldly chided the king to consult the prophets of Ahab and Jezebel and not to expect help from the prophet of the Lord. When Joram was shaken by the letter from the Syrian king requesting Naaman's healing, Elisha sent word to Joram offering his services so that the Syrian captain might "know that there is a prophet in Israel" (II Kings 5:8). Repeatedly Joram was divinely aided through Elisha's ministry in obtaining relief from the Syrian invaders. Elisha faithfully delivered God's message to Joram frequently making predictions and experiencing their fulfillment.

During Joram's reign Elisha extended his ministry to Damascus, the capital of Syria. When Benhadad the Syrian king who was suffering from a serious disease sent his servant Hazael to him to inquire about the prospects for recovery Elisha informed Hazael that the king would die (II Kings 8:10).[5] Subsequently Hazael became king in accordance with what had been revealed to Elijah at Mount Horeb. Elisha's predictions concerning Hazael's oppressive warfare toward the Israelites were also fulfilled during Hazael's reign in Syria (II Kings 10:32–33; 13:3).

Elisha's final mission involving the Omride dynasty was the anointing of Jehu, a son of Jehoshaphat the son of Nimshi, as the king of Israel (II Kings 9). The explicit message through Elisha was that the blood of the servants of God who had been martyred by Ahab would be avenged in the extermination of the royal family together with the Baal zealots. Judgment had been postponed when Ahab repented in response to Elijah's warning (I Kings 21). Mercy had been extended in the ministry of Elisha during Joram's reign but now Jehu was divinely commissioned to execute judgment. Consequently Elijah's prediction concerning Ahab and Jezebel was fulfilled. Even Ahaziah the king of Judah who was the grandson of both Ahab and Jehoshaphat was killed in this judgment.

[5] In the Hebrew of II Kings 8:10 the text reads, "Thou wilt not live," while the Masoretic correction reads, "Thou wilt live." If Elisha said the latter, then Hazael did not tell Benhadad the truth. If Elisha said the former, he must have said it ironically, since the additional statement reflects Elisha's knowledge that Benhadad would die. Cf. C. F. Keil, *The Book of Kings* (Grand Rapids: Eerdmans reprint, 1950), pp. 335–39.

Although Elisha lived throughout the reigns of Jehu and Jehoahaz and died during the rule of Jehoash, *ca.* 798 B.C., nothing is recorded about his activity except the circumstances of his death. The king of Israel was greatly concerned about the loss of this great prophet.

Both Elijah and Elisha were frequently identified as "the man of God." Through their messages and miracles they were acknowledged as God's representatives. Active during a period of excessive apostasy when the royal Omride dynasty was committed to do evil in Israel, these prophets explicitly conveyed God's revelation through the spoken word and mighty acts. Elisha's ministry continued for over four decades after the Omride dynasty was exterminated. Even though Baalism was terminated as the official religion, Jehu failed to provide God-fearing leadership but continued to influence the Israelites in idolatrous ways, ignoring the Mosaic revelation (II Kings 10:31).

RELIGIOUS CONFUSION

Godly leadership and a concern for the Word of God was abruptly terminated in the Southern Kingdom with the death of Jehoshaphat, *ca.* 848 B.C. The consequences of Jehoshaphat's alliance with the Omride dynasty, for which he was severely rebuked by several prophets, came to almost disastrous fruition in the following decade.

Jehoram, the son of Jehoshaphat, was married to Athaliah who apparently was wholly devoted to the Baalism promoted by her parents, Jezebel and Ahab. In killing all his brothers Jehoram exemplified his wickedness, which precipitated judgment in the rebellion of Edom through which the king almost lost his life. Warning came to Jehoram through letters from Elijah the prophet (II Chron. 21:12–15). God's message was explicit. Jehoram's bloodshed and his failure to follow the examples of Jehoshaphat and Asa in providing God-fearing leadership and by contrast his promoting of the idolatrous influence of the Omride dynasty precipitated God's judgment.[6] Subsequently all of Jehoram's sons save Ahaziah were killed. For several of the eight years of his reign he suffered from an incurable disease. When he died the people did not mourn his death, nor did they bury him in the tomb of the kings.

Obadiah, whose message is preserved in the book bearing his name, may have been active during the reign of Jehoram.[7] Edom's successful looting of Judah at this time may have been the basis for her national pride which Obadiah denounced. His assurance that Edom would ultimately be judged from Jerusalem with the Lord as king very likely provided God's word of encouragement for the faithful in Judah during this terrible period of wickedness and idolatry under Jehoram.

The death of Jehoram did not relieve the godless condition in Judah. Ahaziah, son of Jehoram and Athaliah, had ruled but one year when he was killed in Jehu's accession to the throne in Samaria. Athaliah immediately seized the Davidic throne in Jerusalem, attempting to kill all royal heirs as she began her six-year reign of terror. The brothers of Ahaziah had already been taken captive by the Edomites or killed by Jehu in his purge. Joash, an infant son of Ahaziah, however, was saved by Jehosheba, who was a daughter of Jehoram and also the wife of Jehoiada, the high priest. Under Jehoiada's leadership Athaliah was executed and Joash was enthroned at the age of six (II Kings 11; II Chron. 23).

[6] Whether Elijah was still living or whether this verdict on Judah's royal dynasty which was also part of the Omride family was sent to Jehoram by Elisha is not known. Cf. C. F. Keil, *The Books of the Chronicles,* at location.

[7] Although nothing is known about Obadiah, his brief message may be reasonably dated during the reign of Jehoram according to Gleason Archer, *A Survey of Old Testament Introduction* (Chicago: Moody Press, 1964), pp. 287–91.

Jehoiada is not identified as a prophet, nor did he claim to have a new message from God. He was concerned about doing the known will of God as revealed in the Mosaic law and in subsequent writings. Known to him was the simple fact that they as God's covenant people were to have a king of the Davidic lineage and a ruler who was concerned about the vital relationship between his people and God instead of promoting idolatrous Baalism. Jehoiada also supervised the destruction of the Baal shrines, organized the Levites for service, and ruled in behalf of Joash until the young king became of age.

The prophet Joel may be reasonably dated during the early reign of Joash, *ca.* 830 B.C.[8] Joel solemnly warns that divine judgment will be visited upon them in the day of Jehovah. While the locust plague, which was the occasion of his message, inflicted economic losses on Judah the day of judgment would bring destruction upon all nations. As God's messenger, Joel issues a call to repentance with the assurance of God's blessings in material as well as in spiritual provisions before the day of ultimate judgment. Speaking in terms of the contemporary foes of Judah such as the Phoenicians, the Philistines, the Egyptians, and the Edomites, the prophet offers comfort to the people of Judah. The triumph promised over these enemies may have aided the Jews during subsequent periods of threat by these surrounding aggressors. Ultimately God's people will "know that I am the Lord your God dwelling in Zion" when all nations will be subjected to God's rule. Never will they pass through Jerusalem again. Before that final prosperity there will come a manifestation of God's spirit so that "whosoever calls on the name of the Lord will be delivered."[9]

[8] G. L. Archer, *op. cit.,* pp. 292–95, offers an excellent discussion for dating Joel at this time.

[9] Cf. Joel 2:28–32 with Acts 2:14–21. Peter asserts that this prediction was being fulfilled beginning with the events on the day of Pentecost.

As long as Jehoiada lived during the reign of Joash both priest and king were vitally concerned about the man-God relationship. Both exerted leadership in observing the law of Moses, repairing the temple, and replacing genuine worship of God for Baalism. When Jehoiada died, some time after the twenty-third year of Joash's reign, *ca.* 810 B.C., he had gained such recognition for doing "good in Israel, both toward God and toward his house," that he was buried in the city of David among the kings (II Chron. 24:16). After Jehoiada's burial Joash yielded to the pressure of some of his princes in permitting them to break the commandments by substituting idolatry for their devotion to God.

Except for Zechariah the son of Jehoiada (II Chron. 24:19–20), the prophets who testified against these idolatrous leaders are not identified. Empowered by the Spirit of God, this prophet warned that God was forsaking them. Because of this warning, Zechariah was stoned by the princes who influenced the king to issue a decree for execution. The prophet was martyred with the prayer that God would execute vengeance.

King Hazael of Syria was used toward the end of the ninth century to fulfill the prediction made through Elisha (II Kings 8:7–15). Frequently he attacked Jehu and Jehoahaz, devastating the Northern Kingdom east of Jordan as far south as the Arnon Valley (II Kings 10:32–33). Shortly after Zechariah was martyred, the Syrian armies captured Gath and advanced to Jerusalem (II Kings 12:17–18). In desperation Joash sent temple and palace treasures to Hazael to avert a Syrian occupation of Jerusalem. However, a small Syrian army humiliated Judah in executing judgment as the prediction made by Zechariah the prophet was fufilled.

Baalism, after permeating Israel and Judah, left both kingdoms in a very weakened condition. Revolutions in the North in 841 B.C. and in the South in 835 B.C. provided the opportune time for Syrian expansion. During the rest of the ninth century, Syria under its powerful king, Hazael, extended its domination into Judah as well as Israel. After Hazael's death at the turn of the century a new era dawned, first for Israel and later on for Judah.

VI

RELIEF, PROSPERITY, AND CAPTIVITY

WITH THE dawn of the eighth century, relief came to the Southern and Northern Kingdoms in the death of the Syrian king, Hazael, to whom the Israelite kings had repeatedly yielded tribute, captives, and territory. Although Elisha outlived Hazael there is no mention of his activities during the reigns of Jehu and Jehoahaz, *ca.* 841–798 B.C. Release from oppression in answer to the prayer of Jehoahaz (II Kings 13:3–4) may have come with the termination of Hazael's reign, *ca.* 801 B.C. The next king of Israel, Jehoash, expressed genuine concern when he realized that Elisha was on his deathbed. Elisha had an encouraging prediction for the king assuring him of three victories over the Syrian oppressors (II Kings 13:14–25). This was fulfilled when Jehoash recaptured Israelite cities from the control of Benhadad, the new king in Syria.

UNNAMED PROPHETS

Two unnamed prophets delivered pertinent messages to King Amaziah which were crucial to Judah in its effort to regain national strength as Syrian power waned (II Chron. 25). Amaziah was very suddenly enthroned after his father Joash had been wounded by Syrian invaders and assassinated by his servants. As soon as Amaziah was well enough established he mustered an army of 300,000 men to resubjugate Edom which had revolted under Jehoram (II Kings 8:20). After Amaziah hired 100,000 additional soldiers from Jehoash, the king of Israel, a man of God advised him not to enlist the aid of apostate Israel. In addition he assured the king that God's provision would more than duplicate the military aid as well as the price he had paid the king of Israel. With his own army Amaziah defeated Edom.

Upon his return from this decisive victory Amaziah introduced Edomite idolatry into Judah. Subsequently another man of God came to warn Amaziah against breaking God's commandments by bowing to idols. When Amaziah defied this prophet, God's judgment came upon the king through his unwise policy toward Jehoash whose soldiers had pillaged cities after they had been dismissed by Amaziah. In a challenged battle between the North and the South, Amaziah was not only defeated, but Jerusalem was plundered, and he was taken as a prisoner. Fifteen years later he was restored to his throne. Thus the prophecy of this man of God was fulfilled. These developments left Judah in a weakened condition and much inferior to the Northern Kingdom, in spite of the victory over Edom.

JONAH

The prophet Jonah was active in the post-Elisha era. It may have been during Jeroboam's co-regency with his father (*ca.* 793–781 B.C.) that Jonah made the prediction about this king of Israel (II Kings 14:25–27). In subsequent years Jeroboam II (793–753 B.C.) reconquered the territory Israel had previously lost to Hazael and led the Northern Kingdom to an unprecedented peak of political and economic prosperity.

Jonah's mission[1] to Nineveh may be dated in the reign of

[1] Although Curt Kuhl, *The Prophets of Israel* (Richmond, Va.: John

Assyrian kings Adad-Nirari II (810–783 B.C.) or Assurdan III (771–754 B.C.). The account of Jonah's adventures as given in the book bearing his name was probably written by him. Jonah's experience explicitly teaches that God is merciful to heathen nations when they repent. The plagues in Nineveh in 765 and 759 B.C. and the total eclipse of the sun on June 15, 763, probably conditioned the Assyrians for the message of judgment announced by Jonah.[2] The teaching in Israelite law and history that God responded in mercy to those who repent was vividly illustrated in Jonah's life as it applied to the sinful city of Nineveh. His experience had prophetic significance as indicated by Jesus Christ (Matt. 12:40).[3]

Whereas the people of Nineveh repented and turned to God, the Israelites refused to heed the warnings by the prophets during the eighth century. In view of the impending judgment both Amos and Hosea forthrightly admonished their people to repent, abandon their idolatry, and turn to God.

AMOS

By birth Amos was a citizen of the Southern Kingdom, claiming Tekoa, a city five miles southeast of Bethlehem, as his home town. While herding sheep and cultivating sycamore figs he received a divine call to be a prophet (3:8; 7:15). He responded to God's call and proclaimed His message in the Northern Kingdom. The time of his preaching mission is generally dated within the last decade of Jeroboam's reign, *ca.*

Knox Press, 1960), p. 58, recognizes Jonah as historical, he asserts that beyond the reference in II Kings 14:25–27 we know nothing about "the man, who was later mistakenly identified with the minor prophet Jonah (Jon. 1:1) nor about his oracles."

[2] Cf. J. E. Steinmueller, *Companion to Scripture Studies* (New York: Joseph F. Wagner, 1942), Vol. II, p. 289.

[3] For a discussion of various interpretations and dates for the book of Jonah, see G. L. Archer, *A Survey of Old Testament Introduction* (Chicago: Moody Press, 1964), pp. 295–303.

760ff. Although he began his oral ministry two years before the earthquake, the book bearing his name was written later, since he refers to this event as known to his generation. The coming of this earthquake so soon after his solemn warnings of impending judgment may have reminded the Israelites of his message.

The uniqueness and glory of Israel's covenant were clearly seen by Amos (3:2). Boldly he asserted that he did not have any formal training, nor had he attended the school of the prophets so prominent in Elisha's era. The numerous references in Amos to the legal provisions of the Torah indicate that he had read and studied the writings of Moses. These references to the Pentateuch as given by G. L. Archer are:[4]

1. 2:7—Deut. 23:17–18
2. 2:8—Exod. 22:26; Deut. 24:12–13
3. 2:12—Num. 6:1–21
4. 4:4—Deut. 14:28; 26:12
5. 4:5—Lev. 2:11; 7:13

The man-God relationship permeates the entire message of Amos. His appeal to the Israelites is based on their covenant with God and a reminder that they are failing to live up to the requirements expected in this relationship. The repeated references to the law of love for God and for fellow men seem to indicate that they had the Mosaic law as given in the Pentateuch but were neglecting to relate it to daily life. Frequently the history of Israel came into focus as Amos reminded them of God's dealings with them in the past.

Although the message of Amos is given in the Northern Kingdom with application to the particular situation prevailing there, the divine perspective is universal. The temple on Mount Zion is the point at which God enters into the affairs of man-

[4] *Ibid.*, pp. 307–8.

kind (1:2). Israel as a whole is God's covenant people. Although Judah is included with the surrounding nations, there are several additional references which indicate that Judah and Israel are regarded as one in the covenantal relationship with God. The political division is temporal. Judgment is coming to each of the two kingdoms, but ultimately they will be restored as one nation under David (9:11–15).

Amos had relatively little in his message that was new. Taking into account the prevailing social, religious, and political conditions, Amos reminds the Israelites of their sins and predicts coming judgment and restoration. Both national and international history are reflected in the appeal Amos makes to the Israelites.

God's dealings with the surrounding nations in their relationship with Israel are not unique with Amos. When God chose Israel, He dealt with the various nations through Israel, judging Egypt for her oppression (Exod. 4–14), defeating the Amalekites in their attack on Israel (Exod. 17), sparing the Edomites, Moabites, and Ammonites (Deut. 2) but destroying the Amorites and other nations in Canaan whose iniquities had reached the point of judgment in God's economy (Deut. 3:21–22). Amos makes the truth relevant to his generation.

Amos introduces his message to Israel with the announcement that God's judgment is coming upon the surrounding nations because of their offense against Israel (1:3–2:5). Syria, with its capital at Damascus, will be punished for her oppression of Israel in the days of Hazael. The Philistines have sold the Israelites as slaves to the Edomites. The Phoenicians are guilty of taking advantage of Israel in their agreements with Edom. The Edomites will be punished for pursuing the Israelites with the sword. The Ammonites are guilty of cruel warfare against Israel and the Moabites have desecrated the tombs of the Edomite kings. The people of Judah have rejected the law through disobedience, have hardened their hearts and have sinned as their forefathers had done. Amos specifically predicts the destruction by fire of the palaces and forts at Jerusalem.

Israel, however, is due for greater punishment. The reasons are clearly developed. God's grace and goodness had been extended to them in deliverance from Egypt (2:10; 3:1–2, 7), in giving them possession of Canaan (2:9–10), in sending them Nazirites and prophets to warn them (2:11–12), and in sending them drought, famine, crop failure, plagues, and warfare (4:6–11). The Israelites did not respond to these acts of mercy divinely intended to make them God-conscious.

The law of love to God and to fellow men was disregarded by the Israelites in their total pattern of living. Lacking a genuine love for God they were guilty of idolatry and social evils which reflected their failure to love their fellow men. Against the background of Deut. 1–6, Amos denounces the idolatry prevailing at Gilgal, Bethel, Beersheba, Samaria, Dan, and throughout the land of God's covenant people (3:14; 4:4; 5:5–6; 7:9; 8:14). Their devotion to God and worship according to the law is insincere and hypocritical (4:5; 5:21–23; 6:5). They have taken advantage of their fellow men, which was forbidden in the law wherein they were explicitly taught that God was righteous (Deut. 10:17–19). Therefore righteous judgment must reign among the people (Deut. 29:14–21). Justice should prevail in the courts (Lev. 19:35–36; Deut. 16:18–20) and not partiality (Deut. 1:16–17). Amos asserts that the Israelites accepted bribes and sold the poor for a pair of shoes (2:6–7; 4:1; 8:8). Injustice prevails and social evils abound (5:10–12). Cheating in weights is practiced by the merchants (8:5). Practical religion involves both wholehearted devotion to God and love for one's neighbor. Neither the worship of

God nor the consideration of one's fellow man can be neglected in the daily pattern of life.

In addition the Israelites had not heeded God's warnings. They caused the Nazirites to break their vows by drinking wine and they silenced the prophets (2:12). Even Amos was rebuked by Amaziah, a priest at Bethel, who reported to King Jeroboam that Amos was a traitor (7:10–17). Honest judges and those who spoke with integrity were hated (5:10).

Israel's failure to live up to the moral requirements of a God who is perfect in righteousness as had been prescribed in the Torah naturally precipitated judgment. The sovereign God who brought the nations under judgment also brought punishment upon Israel. Moses had warned the Israelites that God's judgment upon other nations for their sinfulness would come upon them if they sinned (Lev. 18:24–30; Deut. 9:4). On the other hand, Amos repeatedly emphasized that the Israelites should prepare to meet God and seek Him (4:12; 5:6, 14–15). That God would be merciful to those who observed the law of love was explicitly stated by Moses in his address to Israel (Deut. 4:29–31).

Amos admonished them to place their trust in God, not in themselves or in their idols. Foolishly they pride themselves on their own power (6:13). Their false glory, their manpower, their beautiful homes, and their cities will all be destroyed.

Amos reminds the Israelites of what God is like even as Moses had done in his generation (Exod. 19–24; Deut. 4–6). God is the God of all nations and chose Israel as His particular interest (Amos 1:1–3:2). God is omnipotent, controlling all nature and then determining famine and plenty (4:1–13 and 5:8). God is omniscient in knowing their thoughts (4:13). He is also a God of mercy (4:11; 7:1–6). Since the relationship between God and His wayward people had been so explicitly delineated in Deut. 4:25ff., Amos emphasized these attributes of God to correct the Israelites' erroneous ideas about Him. Amos also points out that they have not revered God but have profaned His name by immorality (2:7), and have silenced the prophets (2:12). This is the God they should acknowledge in their pattern of living as they prepare to meet Him (4:12).

God's mercy and judgment are vividly portrayed in five visions. Destruction of the surrounding nations is graphically described as a devastation by fire. When God shares with Amos His intent to send swarms of locusts or fire to destroy Israel, the prophet responds with intercession. Mercy is extended and judgment delayed (7:1–6). The third vision portrays God's inspection of Israel and the issuing of the warning that judgment is inevitable (7:7–9). Death was the penalty prescribed by Moses for idolatry (Deut. 7:4). The fourth vision indicates that judgment is near (8:1–2). The fifth vision (9:1–6) depicts the thorough destruction God sends in which no one on earth or heaven will escape.

The predictions concerning Israel's destruction are extensive and detailed. The dynasty of Jeroboam will be destroyed by the sword (7:9). This was fulfilled in 753 B.C. when Zechariah, Jeroboam's son, was killed after a six months' reign (II Kings 15:8–12). The nation will be subjected to an enemy invasion (3:11), which will come from the north and oppress Israel (6:14). Idols and idol shrines will be destroyed (3:14; 7:9). Idolaters will never rise again (8:14). The beautiful homes and palaces they have built will be leveled (6:8–11) and the people will be exiled beyond Damascus (5:27). That this national fate was imminent is indicated in the specific prediction Amos makes concerning Amaziah, the Bethel priest who opposed him (7:17). Amaziah and his children will be killed, his wife will commit adultery, and the Israelites will be taken into captivity. The imminence of their judgment was emphasized through the vision of the basket of summer fruit. Amos also predicts a future famine of God's Word (8:11–13). The predictions of invasion, destruction, and captivity were fulfilled in the coming of the Assyrians, beginning in 745 B.C., who terminated the independence of Syria in 732 and the Northern Kingdom of Israel in 722 B.C.

Like the prophets before him, Amos had a message of hope, which is introduced in the last chapter of the book, where he emphasizes that no one will escape God's judgment. The sinful kingdom will be rooted up and all sinners will perish, but a remnant in Israel will be saved, as indicated by God's use of a sieve. In accordance with the assurance in the Mosaic revelation that God's covenant is eternal and the subsequent promise that David's throne will be established forever, Amos offers the hope that the Davidic kingdom will be restored and raised to a place of superiority over other nations. The fortunes of Israel will be restored so that the people will build cities and inhabit them and enjoy the crops of their vineyards. This prediction (9:11–15) was still awaiting fulfillment when the Jerusalem council convened at the beginning of the Christian era (Acts 15:16–17).

HOSEA

The prophet Hosea likewise expressed a genuine concern about Israel's relationship with God. His ministry began before the reign of Jehu's dynasty was violently terminated in 753 and continued into or even beyond the reign of Hoshea (732–722 B.C.), when overtures were made to Egypt for help against Assyria as is reflected in chapter 7. Consequently his messages were given over a period of three or more decades. Although Hosea may have extended his ministry beyond the fall of Samaria, his book might have been published before the siege of Samaria began in 725 B.C.

Considerable light is shed upon the state of the Northern Kingdom by Hosea. Idolatrous worship and immoral practices were prevalent at various sanctuaries (2:5, 8, 16; 3:1; 4:12–14; 17–18; 10:5–6; 13:2). Lying, perjury, murder, stealing, debauchery, and bloodshed were common (4:1–2; 6:8; 7:1, 5–7; 10:4; 12:7–8). The priests and rulers were guilty of ensnaring and deluding the people in the ways of idolatry (5:1).

The law of love is more elaborately portrayed through Hosea than by any other prophet. This emphasis to apostate Israel in the closing decades of its existence as a kingdom should have made the generation which was about to be absorbed by the Assyrians conscious of God's extended mercy. In deed and in word Hosea communicated to them God's love and pleaded with them to renew their covenant with God.

According to Moses' exposition of the law to the congregation of Israel before his death, love was the keystone in a vital relationship between God and Israel. God's love was expressed in the choosing of the patriarchs and their descendants (Deut. 4:37). Because of this love, God's power was demonstrated in the deliverance of the Israelites from Egypt and therefore Moses admonished the Israelites to acknowledge God (Deut. 4:39) and to love Him (Deut. 6:5). This wholehearted love would find practical expression in a reverence and fear of God which would result in the obeying of His commandments. Since the teaching and observance of the law as well as the experience of learning to fear God was to be taught in the home, this relationship of love became an individual matter (Deut. 6:1–25). Love between God and Israel was essential for the maintenance of the covenant (Deut. 7:6–15). God promised that His love with all its benefits would continue upon those who exhibited a practical expression of love for Him in obeying His commandments (Deut. 10:12–11:31).

Through his marriage and the naming of his children, Hosea

vividly illustrated to the Israelites God's love, which continues even though they do not love Him. The birth of his first son, named Jezreel, precipitated the announcement that God would terminate the Jehu dynasty and the independence of the Northern Kingdom. The name of the second child, Lo-ruhamah, signified that God would be withdrawing His mercy. When the third child was born and named Lo-ammi, Hosea announced that God was disowning His people Israel. When Hosea's wife, Gomer, became disloyal and left him, the message of the prophet was applied to Israel's loving relationship with God. Even as Gomer ignored Hosea and lived an immoral life so Israel had disregarded God through her disloyalty and had turned to sinful ways. Yet, as long as Hosea was active, God's love and mercy continued so that he appealed to them to repent before the coming judgment. Thus his message is crucially relevant.

Hosea explicitly depicts Israel's basic problem. People and priest have rejected the covenant and the law (8:1).[5] The knowledge of God is not among them because they have rejected or nullified this vital relationship and have failed to incorporate the terms of the covenant in their daily lives. Because of the lack of this knowledge they will be destroyed (4:1–11). The knowledge essential for Israel had been revealed in the law and the terms of the covenant. God had made known to

[5] Wellhausen, Marti, and others reflected the nineteenth-century opinion that the Pentateuch was late and therefore Hosea did not have knowledge of the Decalogue. Recently scholars have more widely recognized the Decalogue as dated somewhere between the thirteenth to the ninth century B.C. A. Weiser, *The Old Testament: Its Formation and Development* (New York: Association Press, 1961), asserts that the Decalogue was well established during Hosea's time in the public liturgy of Israel. Others regard this as highly problematic. For discussion, see James M. Ward, *Hosea* (New York: Harper & Row, 1966), pp. 243–45. The context of Hosea's references to the covenant and the law seems to indicate, however, that the Israelites had knowledge of the obligations they had in this covenant relationship as they are delineated in the Pentateuch, especially in the book of Deuteronomy.

Israel His plan (5:9), and the knowledge of God was more important than sacrifice (6:6). An act of involvement, commitment to God by the whole person, was essential as stressed by Moses in Deut. 6:5. This inner dedication to God involved mind, heart, thought, and emotion rather than mere dedication to ceremonies.

The word "know" is used repeatedly by Hosea in his effort to communicate clearly. When he points out that Israel did not know that God provided the crops (2:8), he conveys the important fact that they are not living in accordance with this realization. That God was the sustainer of the universe, providing crops and all material benefits, was known to them through previous revelation. Now they use these crops to make sacrifice to idols. The divine promise is that in the future they shall "know" the Lord (2:20), meaning that they shall sincerely serve Him. Likewise in 11:3 the word "know" signifies realization. Intellectually they were conscious of the fact that God had delivered them from Egypt but they did not act in accordance with this knowledge, ignoring their benefactor. Likewise "I did know thee in the wilderness" (13:5) indicates that God manifested His power in behalf of Israel. The context of the other references (5:3–4; 6:3) also supports the fact that "know" means practical realization of knowledge that is reflected in daily conduct.

Rejection of God's Word and the failure to acknowledge God resulted in the terrible conditions that prevailed (4:1–13). Truth, mercy, and the knowledge of God had been replaced with swearing, lying, killing, stealing and adultery. The priests were guilty of forgetting the law and of approving the sins of the people. Consequently the people were consulting wooden objects used for divination. They were resorting to idolatrous shrines instead of turning to their God. They mingled with the heathen and adopted their ways. The rulers were so sinful that they did not realize that their strength was failing (7:1–10). Instead of turning to God they looked to Egypt and Assyria for help.

Hosea warns them of coming judgment. After the initial announcement of God's judgment in ch. 1 he foretells crop failure and famine (2:1–13). Destruction is coming because the people have failed to keep the law and the covenant (8:1–14). God will terminate His love for them and they shall be scattered among the nations because they have not responded to His gracious dealings with them (9:1–17). God's judgment is sure to come (13:1–3). Samaria must bear her guilt (13:16).

Certain that judgment will come, Hosea offers throughout his sermons a hope of restoration. His messages of coming destruction summarized in ch. 1 include the hope of Israel's regathering (1:10–11). In contrast to the impending destruction and the abandonment of their land to the wild beasts, Hosea assures them of a future state of absolute peace extending even to the animal world (2:14–23), when Israel in reality will be God's people. God's judgment will ultimately be followed by a regathering of His people (11:10). They will be ransomed from the power of death (13:14). God will heal their backsliding and Israel shall no more turn to idols (14:4–9).

Hosea, as God's messenger, is keenly conscious of the fact that God's mercy still prevails as long as he is among them as God's commissioned messenger to warn them. Consequently he makes numerous appeals to his people Israel. He admonishes them to return to God and assures them of God's restoration (6:1–3). If they will plant seeds of righteousness they will reap a crop of God's love and mercy. Theirs is the responsibility to seek after God, since they have been cultivating wickedness and raising crops of sin (10:12–13). Hosea is conscious of God's compassion and love for Israel. In chapter 11 his emphasis shifts from matrimonial love to the compassionate love of a father for his son. God has been a father to Israel, teaching the Israelites to walk, delivering them from Egyptian bondage, and nurturing them in the land of Canaan. Although they are determined to desert God, they will not be completely abandoned in judgment even though this judgment is certain (13:16).

The condition on which God's mercy can be obtained is repentance and confession of sin (14:1–3). By expressing their complete confidence in God through a wholehearted commitment and acknowledging that their trust in Assyria and in their idols is futile, they can renew their covenant with God. This advice was in conformity with that which Moses had prescribed in the book of Deuteronomy. God would respond in mercy to restore them if they repented.

Hosea's warnings were not sufficiently heeded to avert judgment. The prediction that the Northern Kingdom would terminate was fulfilled in 722 B.C. as the Assyrians reduced this kingdom to a province. The Israelites had failed to heed God's law as well as the warnings of the prophets that were sent to them (II Kings 17).

VII

UNDER ASSYRIAN PENETRATION

IN THE wake of the Assyrian advance during the last half of the eighth century, the prophets Micah and Isaiah specifically related God's message to the contemporary scene. Divinely empowered and keenly conscious of the national and international problems facing their leaders in Jerusalem and in Samaria, they boldly warned of God's impending doom upon the two kingdoms and offered a hope for the future.

The messages of Isaiah and Micah can best be understood and interpreted on the assumption that the Israelites had knowledge of the Pentateuch. With this knowledge as a frame of reference the prophets rebuked the Israelites for their failure to live up to the law of Moses, pointed out their responsibility and accountability to God, and warned that judgment and destruction were coming because they had fallen short of God's expectation for His holy people. These prophets were neither innovators nor revolutionists in their prophetic ministry. Repeatedly the basic charges were directly related to the revelation given through Moses.

In reference to the Pentateuch the prophets did not reflect a legalistic attitude. They focused attention primarily upon the relationship of the Israelites with God and the love they were to exercise toward their fellow men. Disobedience was not a matter of legal minutia but was, rather, a sign of laxity in their concern to live in harmony with their total commitment to God. Out of this concern issued love and obedience.

MICAH'S WARNINGS AND HOPES

Micah warns that the Lord God "from his holy temple" is coming with judgment for the Israelites. Life in the capital cities of Samaria and Jerusalem epitomizes lawlessness. God is coming to consume the idols and the shrines. So terrible will be the judgment that surrounding cities are alerted not to mourn for the destruction of God's people.

Justice has decayed. The poor and needy are exploited as rich landowners squeeze out those who cannot pay the exorbitant demands. The court judges abuse their power. Bribery is prevalent. Consequently degradation and widespread misery are the lot of the citizens in the capitals of Israel. Greediness and lust for money have so permeated the life of society that prophets and priests have adapted themselves to favoring the rich and browbeating the poor.

To Micah these evil practices—idolatry, injustice, abuse of the poor, and other religious and political negatives—represented transgressions (1:5). Moses had specifically delineated the responsibilities the Israelites had toward God and toward their fellow men, and had warned them that idolatry and injustice would be punished (Deut. 12ff.).

The Israelites have failed to grasp the meaning of true religion. The bold admonition is that their God, who requires of them love and mercy, is coming in judgment. It was this same God who had shown His mercy to them in redeeming them from Egypt (6:1–10).

The acknowledgment of God as expressed in the First Commandment was to be the guideline. Wisdom in practice was to walk humbly with God and to realize that a righteous God could not tolerate short measures, loaded balances, false weights, violence, and lies (6:11–16). The Israelites were conforming to the rules of Omri and Ahab—leaders committed to idolatrous Baalism—rather than to the instructions given through Moses to those who were committed to love God wholeheartedly. The social evils were symptomatic of a broken relationship with God. The cure was to walk humbly with the God who would be their judge. A renewal of this relationship would automatically remove idolatry and social evils would be replaced by the expression of justice and mercy toward their fellow men, exhibiting God's love to their neighbors. Instead of loving God through their neighbors they would love their neighbors through God.

Judgment is certain. The capital cities of Samaria and Jerusalem will be reduced to desolation as God subjects both kingdoms to foreign invasions. The leaders have failed in their stewardship of leading their citizens in righteous living as prescribed in God's law. Explicitly Micah labels their behavior as sin and transgression (3:8), since they have ignored the standards prescribed in the Mosaic revelation. By these standards they are judged.

While assuring the people that God was with them (3:11), the religious and political leaders continued to be involved in the social injustices and the crimes that prevailed. By their lives they taught the naturalistic conception of God. For all practical purposes the God revealed through Moses was dead and was no longer a living reality. For the sake of these leaders, Zion—the capital hill or the seat of government—would be plowed as a field.

Prospects of restoration are bright. In contrast to the present capital in which social injustice and crime prevail, there is the promise of the re-establishment of Zion. Many nations will look to this restored capital of Israel to learn God's law, which the

Israelites in Micah's time have ignored. Righteous judgment will extend from Zion to the nations far and near. International warfare will cease. Training for war will be abolished and absolute peace will be such a reality that every man will be able to live under the shade of his own vine and fig tree without fear. Whereas people now walk in the name of their idols, God's people then will walk in the name of the Lord their God. This condition will continue forever.

In contrast to the wicked leaders in Micah's time comes the promise of a ruler for Israel whose origin is from ancient times. This ruler is to be born in Bethlehem. Although the Israelites will have been subjected to captivity, dispersion, and suffering under the supremacy of many nations, this ruler will come as a shepherd to care for God's people. He will speak peace, extending his control to the ends of the earth and ensuring absolute security. In this way the vital covenant relationship will be reestablished. God's love for His people will be manifested through supernatural protection and care while they walk and delight in the ways of God.

At that time all the nations fearful of impending judgment shall respect God (7:16–17). Micah repeatedly speaks of a remnant throughout the time of Israel's dispersion—a remnant who will fear and revere God. Confidently the prophet prays with assurance that God will pardon the sins and transgression of the remnant. In view of God's requirements—justice, love, and mercy—Micah had advised the generation in which he lived that they should walk humbly with their God, do justice, and love kindness. To such people God's mercy extends eternally.

ISAIAH

Throughout his long ministry Isaiah expresses a genuine concern about the covenant bond between his people Israel and their God. Repeatedly the expression "my people" occurs in pinpointing this relationship.[1] God is frequently identified as the "Holy One in Israel," which emphasizes His holiness.[2] Instead of living as God's holy people (Exod. 19:1–6), the people of Israel are alienated from Him because of their immoral and idolatrous pattern of behavior.

Apostasy or estrangement from the Holy One of Israel is explicitly depicted in Isaiah's initial message (1:2–4). The Israelites' lack of sensitivity toward a Holy God was evident in their injustice toward the poor, the widows, and the orphans. Love for the stranger and for one's neighbor was missing. These evils were symptomatic of their estranged relationship with God and thus represented legal transgressions.[3] Consequently their offerings and festal observances were merely a ritualistic form displeasing to God as long as social injustice prevailed (1:10–16). In summarizing the outstanding sins which offer clear evidence of their lack of love and wholehearted commitment to God, Isaiah points to their greed, self-indulgence and intemperance, their cynical materialism, their false standards of morality, their intellectual pride and lack of integrity (5:8–23). Repeatedly these sins and transgression are emphasized by Isaiah as he confronts his people with God's message.

Crucial in Isaiah's call to the prophetic ministry was his vision of a holy God who also is identified as the King, the Lord of Hosts. This vision made Isaiah keenly conscious of the vast gap that existed between his sinful people and their holy God. Although the terrible sinfulness of his own generation brought him

[1] The reference "my people" occurs 23 times in Isaiah—11 times in chs. 1–39 and 12 in chs. 40–66. Note also its use by other prophets: Jeremiah—28 times; Ezekiel—20; Hosea—8; Joel—4; Amos—5; Micah—9; Zephaniah—2; Zechariah—2; and Obadiah, once (cf. E. J. Young, *The Book of Isaiah* [Grand Rapids: Eerdmans, 1965], Vol. I, p. 42).

[2] *Ibid.* This occurs 26 times, 12 in chs. 1–39 and 14 in chs. 40–66.

[3] The Hebrew word *pesha* indicates that "transgress" signifies rebellion and the breaking of a legal relationship (cf. G. von Rad, *Theologie des Alten Testaments* (München, 1957), p. 262.

to the point of despair, Isaiah found hope in the atonement God provided for his sin. In this way Isaiah experientially knew of God's exercise of mercy to those who confessed their sinfulness. This personal knowledge enabled him to be a genuine spokesman for God as he warned the people about their estrangement from God and the opportunity to turn to God in repentance. Like Isaiah they too, as individuals in a sinful nation, could experience the genuine forgiveness of sins through confession and repentance. Later this aspect of atonement for sin was more vividly portrayed through the death of the suffering servant.

Impending Judgment

Judgment is certain. A holy God cannot tolerate sin. Unless the people repent, destruction of the kingdom of Judah with its capital, Jerusalem, is coming as God's judgment for their sins (1:27). The execution of God's justice in Zion will necessarily bring judgment for those who have sinned and transgressed. It will simultaneously bring redemption and righteousness for those who repent.

Isaiah never minimizes the impending judgment. Although the Northern Kingdom and Syria fall during his ministry, Isaiah repeatedly predicts that Judah will not be absorbed by the Assyrians. Comparing Assyria to a razor in God's hand, the prophet asserts that Judah will be shaven from head to toe (7:20). In another message he likens the powerful Assyrian advance to a river that will submerge Judah to its neck (8:7–8), but in neither case does he predict Judah's destruction by the Assyrians. Neither the razor nor the river brings with it terminal judgment for the kingdom of Judah.

Later in his ministry Isaiah assures Hezekiah that the Assyrians will not conquer Jerusalem (37:5–7; 37:21–35). Isaiah does warn the king subsequently, however, that the exile for Judah will come through the Babylonians (39:5–8). Although God's mercy is extended during Hezekiah's time, exilic judgment is certain to come during subsequent generations.

The foreign nations which were temporarily being used by God to bring judgment upon Judah would ultimately be destroyed. Assyria was the rod of God's anger (10:5). The God who used Assyria to bring about the destruction of Samaria with her idols would also bring about the downfall of Assyria (10:10–19). Assyria's strength and wisdom would fail her in the display of God's power.

Babylon is represented by Isaiah not only as the apex of world power but also as the center of idolatry (13:1–24:27; 21:1–10). This spirit of world power directed against God is to be cut off in judgment. Numerous other nations surrounding Judah will also be cut off (chs. 15–23).

This panoramic view of judgment seems to be enlarged to a worldwide perspective in Isaiah's message in chapter 24. Whereas 24:1–13a may be limited in its interpretation to the devastation of Judah and Jerusalem, the remaining part apparently includes judgment for the kings of the earth on a universal basis.

Hope beyond Judgment

The hope of restoration and future glory is more extensively portrayed by Isaiah than by any other prophet. The promise of redemption subsequent to judgment appealed only to the God-fearing element among the Israelites. The others, who were not willing to confess their sins and repentantly turn to God, did not believe that judgment was coming; thus the promise of restoration did not have any real significance for them.

The assurance of restoration was given against the background of a literal destruction of the kingdom of Judah and Jerusalem. In contrast to ruins and exile there came the prospect of a reestablished Zion to which all nations would look for directions (2:1–5). In this triumphant state of God's kingdom absolute peace and righteousness would prevail so that war would be completely abolished. The knowledge of God would permeate the entire world. Israel would be reinstated to her place of prominence among the nations (11:10–16).

Restoration hopes are again delineated after a prayer of praise for God's past judgments (25:6–12; 27:12–13). The conditions of perfect justice and blessing as God's glory and majesty permeate the kingdom are vividly portrayed in chapter 35. God's ransomed people shall rejoice in Zion.

Although there are repeated references in Isaiah 40ff. to Zion's redemption, the climax to this grand theme is provided in chapters 60–66. Nations and kings shall come to Zion bringing their wealth and acclaim to the people who once were oppressed and exiled. The new heaven and the new earth will provide the place of ultimate bliss for those who fear God and are identified as the servants of the Lord.

The Messiah

The promise for Israel's restoration was vested in a person who in subsequent literature is commonly identified as the Messiah. Throughout Isaiah the characteristics of this individual make it apparent that he is a unique person who will be able to establish and rule a kingdom that will endure forever. Consequently Isaiah repeatedly appeals to his people to maintain a relationship of confidence and trust in God.

The ultimate kingdom was projected in contrast to the doomed kingdom existing in Isaiah's time. The Messiah as the coming ruler was usually portrayed in contrast to the local king. Uniquely apparent in Isaiah's book is the ministry and identification of this coming king as the suffering servant.

To the survivors in Israel (4:2), Isaiah promises that they

will find beauty, pride, and glory in the "branch of the Lord" and the "fruit of the land." This seems to identify an individual whose origin is uniquely "of the Lord" and "of the land," representing respectively the divine and the human.[4]

In confrontation with King Ahaz, the prophet Isaiah spoke of the birth of a child named Immanuel, meaning "God with us." This represented a contrast to the godless Ahaz who promoted idolatry in the temple area instead of exemplifying a wholehearted love for God as was expected of him as king. Isaiah's use of *almah* as the mother of this Immanuel must have been significantly suggestive of the unique origin of this son whose name should have brought a consciousness of God's presence.[5] Since neither Isaiah nor Ahaz—nor anyone else as far as our knowledge of that period extends—had a son named Immanuel, it is reasonable to interpret this promise as identifying a future ruler. Significantly the land of Palestine is called the land of Immanuel (8:8). Although Matthew quotes Isaiah 7:14 in reference to the birth of Christ, the son born to Mary is named not Immanuel but Jesus. Consequently the time when Israel's ruler will be known as Immanuel still seems to be in the future.

[4] Cf. E. J. Young, *op. cit.*, pp. 172–182, and J. A. Alexander, *Commentary on the Prophecies of Isaiah* (Grand Rapids, Mich.: Eerdmans, 1953), pp. 121–124.

[5] Cf. E. J. Young, *op. cit.*, pp. 286–89. Evidence is lacking for using *almah* to identify a married woman. In Gen. 24:43, however, *almah* explicitly identifies Rebekah as a virgin. Even though the word *almah* may not be regarded by many scholars and linguists as identifying a virgin, the name "Immanuel" in this same verse alerted Isaiah's listeners to the hope that in this child would be the manifestation of God's presence in a peculiar capacity. This verse (7:14) is more fully understood in 9:6–7 where the child which is born is explicitly identified as "the Mighty God," a term never applied to a mere human being.

Vischer in *Die Immanuel Botschaft in Rahmen des königlichen Zionsfestes* (Zollikon-Zurich, 1955) mentions that Luther offered a hundred *Gulden* to anyone who could provide a reference in which *almah* identified a married woman.

The ruler of the ultimate kingdom which will endure forever is identified as a descendant of David (9:6–7). Born as a child or son in the human race he is described as "Wonderful Counselor, Mighty God, Everlasting Father, Prince of Peace." Most significantly this individual is equated with "Mighty God," providing the most explicit affirmation in the Old Testament of the deity of the coming ruler. At the same time the context indicates that he is born into the human race. The balance of the human and the divine origin emphasizes the uniqueness of this God-Man whose coming is promised.

This coming ruler is vividly described in Isaiah 11:1–11. As is suggested by the figures of "shoot" and "branch," this coming king will emerge from the line of Jesse, the father of David. His characteristics definitely exceed those of any human being. Whereas Ahaz has defied God's message through Isaiah and has used his own wisdom in seeking to solve international problems,[6] this ruler will be filled with the Spirit of the Lord, demonstrating wisdom, insight, wise decisions, and the power to execute them. In fact, he will exemplify a truly God-fearing person. Out of this vital relationship with God issues the capacity to project justice to mankind reflecting God's love, mercy, and justice. The poor and needy will receive fair treatment under his jurisdiction, while the merciless and wicked will be judged. Absolute justice will prevail. Peaceful conditions will permeate even the animal world. This ruler will be endowed with unprecedented power so that the social gospel will be fully realized.

This ruler of Jesse's lineage will not only rule in Zion where the God-fearing survivors will gather, but knowledge of the

[6] Cf. S. J. Schultz, *The Old Testament Speaks* (New York: Harper & Row, 1960), pp. 196–99, 208–9, 306–13, for the historical background and context in which Isaiah delivered these messages to King Ahaz and citizens of Judah.

Lord shall extend throughout the earth. Nations from afar shall rally and turn to him for consultation.

A "cornerstone in Zion" is another designation for the Messiah in Isaiah's prophetic message (28:16). In all likelihood this message is addressed to Ahaz and his counselors who had successfully made an alliance with the king of Assyria as seems to be reflected in the context. Isaiah warns that their treaty will not be sufficient to spare them from divine judgment. The cornerstone, which is described as precious, well tested, solid, and secure, is posited as a person in whom men can trust in full confidence so that they will never be in haste or be ashamed. Again the divine origin is indicated in the Word of the Lord God, "I lay in Zion. . . ." Whereas Isaiah's people trust in Ahaz, the appeal here is for them to place their faith in the person whom God will raise up in Zion. For the God-fearing people this provides a hope in the face of impending judgment. Whereas the people who placed their faith in Ahaz will be disappointed, the divine promise is that those who place their faith in this God-sent person will never need to make haste or be ashamed.

The rule of a righteous and just ruler is again projected by Isaiah in ch. 32. Although some expositors would limit this reference to Hezekiah, it is doubtful that the conditions described here were fully realized under his rule. Thus another promise is given that a righteous ruler will come to execute perfect righteousness.

Having explicitly predicted the exile of his people Israel in chapter 39, Isaiah portrays the Messiah as the suffering servant. Through Him hope is provided for their future salvation (chs. 40–53).

Israel's relationship with God has been completely broken. Not only have they failed to serve God wholeheartedly, but in addition they have turned to idolatry which has precipitated divine judgment. Consequently they have utterly failed in their mission as God's servants to bring justice to the nations. In contrast to Israel's failure as a servant, Isaiah described God's ideal servant in 42:1–4. This one is endued with God's Spirit so that he will establish justice, extending God's law to the coastlands. God's servant is commissioned to restore Israel to be a light to the nations so that God's salvation will reach to the ends of the earth (49:6–7). Even though this servant is to be subject to rulers he will ultimately be exalted to receive the homage of kings. This promise occurs again in 52:13.

Whereas Israel's love relationship with God has resulted in divorcement through her disobedience (50:1–3), the perfectly obedient individual[7] described in the subsequent verses (4–9) emerges in chapter 53 as the righteous servant who suffers for the sins of others. Through his vicarious sacrifice this servant fulfills the mission of atoning for the sins of Israel as well as of the Gentiles. Through this righteous servant many shall be justified so that the temple shall be made a house of prayer for all people (56:1–8).

The absolute necessity for an intercessor such as the Messiah is emphasized once more in chapter 59:15bff. Israel as a nation had failed as God's servant to accomplish the mission assigned to her.[8] Furthermore, not an individual could be found in Israel who was righteous and capable of bringing in justice. Through God's provision this mission is accomplished in the coming of the God-sent Redeemer to Zion. Not only does the

[7] For summary of various interpretations of the "servant," see J. A. Alexander, *op. cit.,* at reference. The servant described here seems to exceed the characteristics ascribed to any man.

[8] Johannes Blauw, in his book *The Missionary Nature of the Church* (New York: McGraw-Hill, 1962), points out that "Israel has been called in her election by Yahweh to be preacher and example, prophet and priest for the nations" (p. 28). In the realistic sense, however, Israel was "itself too strongly inclined to heathen practices to be a clear witness in the world of its day" (p. 17).

Redeemer bring salvation to his own people Israel, but redemption is extended to include the Gentiles so that they could be included in the worship at Zion (60:1–62:12).

Isaiah's Practical Appeal

Having portrayed the suffering servant through whom atonement was made possible for those who accepted God's way as outlined in chapter 55, the prophet now distinguishes between those who fear God and those who ignore Him. Even though the nation as a whole is under condemnation, individual Israelites can qualify as God-fearing people who are identified in Isaiah 54–66 as God's servants. Through a right relationship with God they can be enabled to exercise a relationship with their fellow men that is pleasing to God and thus can be the inheritors of the restored kingdom. By contrast, those who do not foster a genuine wholehearted acknowledgment of God and consequently do not have the capacity to treat their fellow men with compassion and love will ultimately be rejected by God and subjected to eternal separation from God's mercy. Thus concludes the message of Isaiah in chapters 56:9–66:24.

Isaiah graphically describes the people who violate the basic commandments, neglecting love for God and for their fellow men. The religious and political leaders are charged with greediness, lack of compassion for the righteous who are oppressed, participation in idolatry and its rites; and in addition they lack the fear of God (56:9–57:12). The iniquities and sins of the people have separated them from God. Having turned from their devotion to God they are confused about justice and truth (59:1–12). Revolt, bloodshed, evil, iniquity, and strife permeate their pattern of living.

The religious rites and ceremonies likewise are displeasing to God. Seeking Him daily in fasting and prayer is not acceptable to God if they continue in their evil ways of oppressing the poor or if they fail to provide help for the needy (58:1–7). The prayer recorded in 63:7–64:12 seems to express the sentiment and attitude of a self-righteous remnant. They seem to demand that God must act in their behalf because they are descendants of Abraham (63:15–16). They apparently blame God for their hardened hearts and their lack of fear for Him (63:17). They assume that since God is their Father and they are God's chosen people He won't restrain Himself but will deliver them (64:8–12).

God's answer, however, seems to be one of rejection (65:1–7). God had dealt with them in mercy but they had rejected Him. They had rebelled and continued in their evil ways. Now they would be judged for having spurned Him in the day of mercy.

The characteristics of the people pleasing to God are likewise described. Frequently they are identified as God's servants, beginning in chapter 54:17. Promised an ultimate inheritance in God's holy mountain, these people, who put their trust in God and reflect an attitude of contrition and humility, are assured of God's indwelling presence, peace, and healing for the present life (57:13–21).

Special promises are made to those who terminate oppression, abstain from a scornful attitude and slanderous speech, feed the hungry, and help the afflicted. These people also keep God's holy day or Sabbath as a delight with a profound reverence for Him rather than as a mere legalistic observance (58:8–14). People conforming to God's will in this pattern of living are assured of His presence and divine guidance. Their lives will flourish like a watered garden so that they will be known for their constructive influence as it relates to their fellow men.

The summary description of the man pleasing to God is expressed in chapter 66:2b. Basically important is the qualification of humility. A man with a contrite spirit attracts the personal attention of Almighty God who uses heaven as His throne and the earth as His footstool. "Trembling at God's Word" is the second qualification for pleasing Him. Reflected in this attitude are awe and reverence for God. Consequently a right relationship of love and respect for God inherently produces an eagerness to execute God's instructions for daily living.

Isaiah's conclusion is clearly stated (65:1–66:24). Judgment awaits the wicked. Everlasting blessing is provided for God's servants. The disobedient are eternally separated from God's mercy while the obedient are the inheritors of God's everlasting blessing in the new heaven and the new earth. Thus the grand theme of Isaiah's prophecies is brought to a climax in the ultimate hope for the people who are concerned about a right relationship with God. It is the man who loves God wholeheartedly who has a genuine love and compassion for his fellow human beings. These true servants of God are given the assurance that God's mercy will be extended to them without end.

VIII

MERCY BEFORE JUDGMENT

THE GREATEST judgment upon the nation of Israel in Old Testament times was the destruction of Jerusalem by the Chaldeans in 586 B.C. From the human perspective the national hopes of Israel seemed to be entirely extinguished with the burning of the temple and the razing of the capital. The prophets, however, as spokesmen for God offered the hope of restoration beyond the impending doom of their contemporary kingdom.

NAHUM

Nahum, whose ministry is reasonably dated after the fall of Thebes *ca.* 662 B.C. and before the destruction of Nineveh in 612 B.C., has a vital interest in the relationship between God and the powerful nation of Assyria. Jerusalem had been miraculously spared conquest as the kings of Assyria extended their control down into Egypt. Even though the Ninevites of Jonah's time had repented, the Assyrians during Nahum's era were known as a God-defying people noted for their brutality in trampling down weaker nations. How long would a holy and just God tolerate this?

Though long-suffering, a just, holy, and incredibly powerful God executes justice on the wicked. Hope is provided in the assurance that God knows those who trust in Him (1:7). Concerned with Judah's relationship with God, Nahum reminds his fellow Israelites of their vows. They should observe their festivals with rejoicing and thanksgiving that the harassment by the cruel invaders had come to its end through the judgment of a holy and just God (1:15).

The vivid portrayal of Nineveh's destruction conveys the reality of Assyria's passing power, which fades under divine judgment. For their cruelty and injustice they are judged and punished.

HABAKKUK

The injustice prevailing among his own people caused the prophet Habakkuk much anxiety. In his prayers he complains about the murder, bribery, oppression, fighting, and arguing which prevail while the righteous suffer. It may have been after the untimely death of Josiah in 609 B.C., when even Jeremiah was subjected to suffering under corrupt political and religious leaders, that Habakkuk impatiently questioned God's relationship to these prevailing evil conditions among his people.

When God replies with the assurance that the Chaldeans will invade, bringing judgment upon the Israelites, the prophet is shocked. How can a just God permit a pagan nation to judge His own people, however idolatrous they may be? Although puzzled by this divine tolerance of increased wickedness, the prophet is entrusted to write the answer. Whatever may happen, one thing is certain: "The righteous shall live by his faith" (2:1–4). Ultimately God will destroy the wicked and the idolaters. God is in His holy temple and all the earth ought to keep silence before Him who is in control.

This book exemplifies Habakkuk's personal faith in God and hope for the future. In his psalm of praise, Habakkuk resolves his difficulties with utmost confidence in the living God.[1] Even though present circumstances are totally against him, ultimate triumph is certain. In this way Habakkuk finds a solution to his problem through wholehearted confidence in God, who will right the social evils over which Habakkuk has no control.

ZEPHANIAH

With clarity and boldness Zephaniah announces the doom of Judah and Jerusalem. Instead of maintaining a vital relationship with God, the people have failed to seek Him (1:6) and have transgressed in turning to idolatry. Some have tried to serve both the Lord God and the Ammonite god Milcom at the same time (1:5).

Although Zephaniah issues a call to repentance (2:1–3), the prevailing unethical and immoral practices reflect a broken relationship with God (3:1–7). Consider the charges against them: disobedience, refusing correction, lack of trusting and seeking after God, pollution of the sanctuary by prophets and priests who have refused to observe the law, and corruption by political leaders. Their failure to love God has resulted in prevailing evils toward their fellow men. For ignoring God, the Israelites will be subjected to captivity. Finally God's judgment will come upon all nations.

Ultimate restoration is promised. A remnant willing to trust God will experience restoration when the King of Israel returns to Zion. God's people will be gathered from every land.

[1] Although the absence of the third chapter from the First Qumran Cave Commentary on Habakkuk was regarded by some critics as supporting the theory that Habakkuk did not write this chapter, recent critics, according to Gerhard von Rad, suggest that this theophany described in chapter 3 should also be considered (cf. *Old Testament Theology, op. cit.,* Vol. II, p. 190. For a discussion of the authorship of Habakkuk, see G. L. Archer, *A Survey of Old Testament Introduction* (Chicago: Moody Press, 1964), pp. 344–45.

This is the ultimate hope beyond the judgment precipitated by their wickedness. In the meantime, while the prophet is proclaiming God's message, God's mercy is extended toward the generation in which Zephaniah lives until Jerusalem is actually conquered in divine judgment.

JEREMIAH

During the last forty years of Judah's existence as a kingdom, Jeremiah was active in Jerusalem (626–586 B.C.). As God's messenger he witnessed the great reformation and revival under Josiah as well as the disintegration of the kingdom to the point of utter destruction under Zedekiah. Living under the shadow of approaching judgment, Jeremiah devotes most of his time to warning the people that they must mend their ways in order to avert or postpone Jerusalem's destruction as long as God's mercy is extended to them. Restoration hopes are given brief but very definite consideration.

The core of Israel's problem, says Jeremiah, is cultic apostasy —they have forsaken God (2:13). More than any other prophet, Jeremiah speaks of this broken relationship with God.[2] Repeatedly he enumerates substitutions that have been made for the wholehearted commitment and love emphasized by Moses. Having forsaken God who is the fountain of living waters, they have hewed out cisterns which are broken and can hold no water.

Israel has ignored God's love which was lavished upon her in her redemption from Egypt and her settlement in Canaan and has sinned in turning to idolatry. The priests have failed in leading the people back to God, the teachers of the law have no vital relationship or contact with God, the rulers themselves

[2] G. von Rad points out that Jeremiah gives much less space to "reproof for breaking legal enactments than to complaints against Israel's cultic apostasy" (cf. *op. cit.*, p. 194).

are transgressors, and prophets, instead of representing God, are identified with Baal and idolatry. Israel has been divorced from her God. The people lack the fear and reverence for God they should exemplify as His holy people. They have failed to love God and consequently have failed to love their fellow man. All other laws are insignificant when love for God and neighbor is neglected.

Can divorced Israel renew her vows with her God? Jeremiah sees his people plunging toward judgment. In a graphic description the prophet warns his people that God's judgment is certain and imminent. Although he warns them to repent, he realizes that this divine judgment is coming very soon (4:5–6:30).

This broken relationship with God had led to numerous irregularities in their daily pattern of living (7:1–11:23). Legalism, religious formalism, and ritualistic observance of the law seemed to be the order of the day. From Jeremiah's messages it is apparent that Israel trusted in the temple, confident that God would not permit His holy place of worship to be destroyed (7:1). The people were certain that as custodians of the law they were safe (8:8). Presumptively they counted on God's covenant with them, but Jeremiah boldly charged them with their failure in obeying the terms of this relationship. Pointing to the ruins of Shiloh, where the tabernacle was located in the days of Joshua and Eli, he warned that Jerusalem would be subjected to the same fate.

The law in the hands of the scribes and priests has been misused. The external formalities in worship and service can never save them from judgment. While the people ritualistically worship God in the temple, they simultaneously worship idols everywhere—idols so numerous that they have one for each street in Jerusalem and one for each city in the kingdom of Judah.

True religion is lacking. Not knowing God and not exhibiting a wholehearted love for Him, they are far from demonstrating God's love to their fellow men (9:2–7). Instead of loving their neighbors, the generation of Jeremiah's time is guilty of sins of the tongue: slander, lies, deceitfulness, and crafty cunning. Falsehood instead of faithfulness is the law of the land. Through cheating and trickery they take advantage of each other. Oppression is prevalent. There is no such thing as neighborly love. They have no desire to reform their conduct. Greediness, injustice, immorality, murder, and theft are so commonly practiced among them that the offenders feel no shame. Immorality is a concomitant with idolatry (5:1–9; 7:3–11; 23:10–14) for Jeremiah's generation. Moral corruption is inescapable when the fear of God and reverence for His laws are eliminated.

The religious leaders composed of priests and prophets supported the populace in opposition to Jeremiah and the Mosaic revelation. Jeremiah was stunned and horrified that the prophets prophesied falsely and the priests taught according to their own standards with the popular support of the people (5:30–31). With the religious leaders guilty of greediness and deceit, falsely assuring the people of peace (6:13–14), misinterpreting the law (8:8–12), misleading the people by claiming to prophesy in God's name (14:13–16), and living in sinful conditions comparable to those of Sodom and Gomorrah, it was apparent that judgment must come (23:9–40). Jeremiah was heart-broken about this condition even though the people repeatedly countered his message as he continued to warn them.

With the temple and Jerusalem about to be destroyed, Jeremiah pressed the importance of each individual's moral and spiritual relationship with God. Confidence should not be fixed in the temple, sacrifices, the priesthood, the Ark which symbolized God's presence, knowledge of the law, circumcision, or the covenant. Jeremiah did not oppose the observance of the rites and ceremonies prescribed by the law but, like Moses in Deut. 10:16 and 30:6, he insisted that circumcision of the heart (4:4; 9:26) is essential for those who love God wholeheartedly. Knowledge of the written law is useless unless the law is inscribed on the heart. An inward faith in God, a profound reverence for His law, and a willing obedience expressed in love and devotion—these were essential features of a religion pleasing to God.

With clarity Jeremiah delineates between the individual who pleases God and the person whom God rejects (17:1–18). Sin, engraved on the horns of the altar, is but an expression of what is in the heart of man, the heart being the center and fountainhead of life. The outward actions—treachery, deceit, idolatry, hypocrisy, and all the sins so frequently pinpointed by Jeremiah—are but the fruits or outward expression of a deceitful and corrupt heart. The verdict is that any individual who has confidence in himself and turns away from God is cursed. Like a tree in the desert he has no hopeful prospects for the future. The heart is the source of sin. Judgment in destruction and captivity is inevitable. Those who trust in man instead of in God will ultimately be put to shame.

By contrast the man pleasing to God is the individual who places his confidence or trust in Him. A wholehearted commitment, faith, and love directed Godward instead of toward sinful self will result in fruitfulness throughout the difficulties of life. Like a tree, which has a good water source, bears fruit even in times of drought, so the individual, whose trust and confidence is in God, will prosper.

The Promise of Restoration

Although Jeremiah was moved to tears as destruction and captivity neared reality, he prayed earnestly, hoping judgment would be postponed or averted. God, however, repeatedly commanded him not to pray—it was too late for prayer. The time had come that Moses (Exod. 32:11; Num. 14:13–20) and Samuel (I Sam. 7:9; 12:23)—conspicuous examples of the power of intercessory prayer—would only save themselves through prayer. Jeremiah's celibacy was to serve as a continual reminder to the people that judgment was coming during his lifetime.

As the Judean kingdom disintegrated under the encroaching advance of the Babylonians, Jeremiah specifically projected the hope for those in exile as it related to their questions and problems. Shortly after some Judean hostages were taken captive to Babylon in 605 B.C., Jeremiah provided a realistic hope in the assurance that after seventy years the captives would return (ch. 25). Speaking about God's judgment as a cup of wrath, Jeremiah pointed out that God was bringing evil upon Jerusalem. Subsequently this cup would be given to surrounding nations. Thus he advised that they should submit themselves to the Babylonian ruler and that resistance was futile.

After the extensive exilic exodus from Jerusalem in 597 B.C., Jeremiah sent letters to the exiles who were impatiently hoping to return at an early opportunity, since they did not believe that Jerusalem would be destroyed. Jeremiah's advice was that they should settle in Babylonia, plant vineyards, and build houses because the captivity would last seventy years.

A greater restoration than the return from Babylon is promised by Jeremiah. With more forceful and explicit statements than any other prophet had made, he asserts that Israel's kingdom will be restored in the regathering of the Israelites from the ends of the earth (chs. 30–33). At least part of this message was given when the armies of Babylon were besieging Jerusalem before its fall in 586 B.C.

When the fall of Jerusalem seemed to be inevitable even to those who had so far refused to believe God's message, Jeremiah was instructed to purchase property as a sign of future restoration. Although he had specifically predicted a return after seventy years, these chapters focus attention primarily upon the ultimate return in the final regathering of Israel. As God had watched over them in their dispersion so He would direct them in their return.

The conditions prevailing in this restored state stand in contrast to the disintegration of the temporal kingdom. A branch of righteousness of Davidic seed shall rule, executing righteousness throughout the land. A new covenant will be established—unlike the previous one which the Israelites had broken through their disobedience. God's law will be inscribed on their hearts so that in practice they will be His people. Each individual will know God with a consciousness of sins forgiven. Gathered in Zion in a state of absolute peace, God's people will rejoice and prosper.

The core of Jeremiah's message seems to be summarized in 9:23–24. Wisdom, power, and riches accrued by man are but temporary sources of security, whereas from the eternal perspective it is God who exercises love, justice, and righteousness. Consequently, the one who maintains a relationship with God is justified in boasting. Jeremiah is confident that the person who responds responsibly to God's love will not need to fear the execution of God's justice and righteousness. When the true and living God who is the King of Israel as well as the King of all nations will punish the uncircumcised, even the Israelites will be judged for their uncircumcision of the heart (9:25–10:16). Those, however, who know God properly and in obedience maintain the covenant relationship are among those who belong to and are identified with the Lord of Hosts. Conscious of the temporality of all things in this life and the ultimate judgment of God, Jeremiah was concerned that each man should have a proper knowledge of Him.

EZEKIEL

In Ezekiel's approach to his generation the relationship between the Israelites and their God had been broken. They were a rebellious people who had already been exiled.

Divinely commissioned to be a watchman, Ezekiel was sent to his own fellow exiles. Although removed from Palestine they shared the conviction of Jeremiah's audience that Jerusalem would not be destroyed. Consequently they falsely hoped to return to Jerusalem at the earliest opportunity.

Ezekiel's charge was simple and direct. The Israelites had failed to obey and had even scorned God's requirements of them in their covenant relationship. They had not lived as God's holy people (5:6). They had defiled the sanctuary, even including idolatry in their religious life.

Unique in Ezekiel's message is the vivid portrayal of God's glory which represented His presence among His people. Theologically correct were those who maintained that the temple in Jerusalem was God's dwelling place even as the tabernacle had been previously since the Sinai revelation under Moses. When Solomon dedicated the temple, the people witnessed the manifestation of God's glory which filled the temple (II Chron. 7:1–3). In the vision (Ezek. 8–11), which Ezekiel shared with the elders in exile, he dramatically portrayed the departure of God's glory or presence from the temple. God abandons the temple as well as the city to utter destruction.

The reasons for this drastic judgment are clearly stated. The sanctuary of God had been defiled: elders tolerated, approved, and participated in idolatry; the women were weeping to the foreign god Tammuz in the gate of the Lord's house; and twenty-five leading men were worshiping the sun with their backs to the temple. Acknowledgment of God's presence and true worship had been replaced by blatant idolatry. Bloodshed and injustice permeated their daily lives while love and respect for each other were conspicuously absent. God's fury and wrath are now due upon the Israelites for their evil deeds (5:12–17; 9:9–10).

The relationship between the individual and God is significantly emphasized by Ezekiel as the nation of Israel is subjected to God's wrath in the razing of the temple, the destruction of Jerusalem, and the exile of the populace. The soul that sinneth shall die (18:20) is the timely warning. The wicked will not be saved because of the presence of the righteous, nor will the righteous perish with the wicked in judgment. In God's perfect justice each individual will receive his just dues.[3]

Mercy preceded this great outpouring of God's wrath. Repeatedly Ezekiel warned the people to repent (cf. 14:6–11), even as prophet after prophet had done in times past and as Jeremiah was doing in Jerusalem until the actual destruction occurred. Even in the execution of divine judgment the individuals who "sign and groan over all the abominations" (9:4) that prevailed in Jerusalem were carefully marked and spared. In this way the God-fearing individuals continued to be favored with His everlasting mercy.

"Harlotry" epitomized the relationship between God and the Israelites in the message of Ezekiel (23:1–49). Samaria had been untrue to God and had courted Assyrian favor, but subsequently the people of the Northern Kingdom had been exiled to Assyria. Jerusalem, which had survived Assyrian might

[3] Individualism was stressed by Moses as he delineated the terms of the covenant (Deut. 4–11). Wholehearted devotion to God by Israel as a nation was dependent upon the individuals being faithful in their relationship. Parents were charged in their family units to teach each child to "fear and revere God." When national existence in its political and religious forms is about to culminate in God's judgment of destruction and dispersion, Ezekiel focuses particular attention upon the individual. The direct relationship of each life with God becomes more crucially important when Israel's national hopes disappear.

through God's providential care, incurred double guilt. For her idolatrous ways Jerusalem was doomed for destruction by the Babylonian kingdom.

Hope is expressed in the tender relationship of a shepherd and his sheep after the destruction of Jerusalem actually occurs (Ezek. 34). False shepherds had influenced the Israelites to deviate from their wholehearted commitment to God and had led them to national ruination as Moses had forewarned them (Lev. 26:14–23). Now God, as the Great Shepherd, promises ultimate restoration, which is portrayed in the Davidic ideal. Ezekiel explicitly predicts that this kingdom will be restored.

Exiled to the ends of the earth for their sins, the Israelites are to be regathered. This is vividly portrayed in the vision of the valley of dry bones. Even as these bones supernaturally take on life, so the Israelites are to be gathered and restored as a nation. Challenged by a northern confederacy, they will ultimately be re-established in their own land. The presence of God will be manifest among them as the glory of God once more fills the temple.

Repeatedly the relationship between God and the Israelites is expressed in the statement, "They shall know that I am the Lord."[4] Although they had intellectual and theological knowledge about God based on the Mosaic revelation, Ezekiel's people did not live in accordance with a realistic awareness of what God was like. If they ignored the warning of the prophets, continued to rebel, and failed to repent, then God's judgment executed upon Israel would bring them to the realization that God is just and righteous, punishing sin (5:13–16:13). Through these developments the Israelites would acknowledge God as they endured the consequences of having previously ignored His love and mercy.

[4] These words occur 86 times in Ezekiel. For discussion see W. Zimmerli, *Erkenntniss Gottes nach dem Buche Ezekiel* (Zurich, 1954), pp. 65ff.

Now Israel would also know God in His everlasting mercy. When they are regathered from exile, the Israelites as well as the heathen will realize what God is like (36:21–38). In their national revival and the establishment of the kingdom, the Israelites will in reality "know that I am the Lord."

IX

RESTORATION HOPES

TO THE exiles who maintained a vital relationship with God, the promises of restoration must have been the basis of their future hope. In addition to the assurances of return from exile as outlined by Moses in the Pentateuch there were the writings of the prophets. Assuming they had the scroll of Isaiah as well as that of Jeremiah the God-fearing Israelites must have found comfort in the promise of restoration or return to their own land under Cyrus. In due time a remnant of the exiles returned, in 539 B.C., and rebuilt the temple in 520–515 B.C., stimulated and encouraged in their work by the prophets Haggai and Zechariah. The final prophetic message came in the last half of the fifth century through the prophet Malachi.

DANIEL

The most detailed and extensive perspective of international developments as related to the Jewish nation came in the revelation to the prophet Daniel.[1] Taken as a royal hostage to

[1] For a consideration of viewpoint that Daniel was the author of this book bearing his name, see Gleason Archer, *A Survey of Old Testament Introduction* (Chicago: Moody Press, 1964), pp. 365–88. For an interpretation of the book of Daniel as a literary unit composed by an unknown Jew after

Babylon in 605 B.C., he rose almost immediately to a top administrative post under Nebuchadnezzar. Although he possibly was inactive under subsequent rulers, he was promised third place in the Babylonian kingdom on the eve of Babylon's conquest by Cyrus. In the Medo-Persian kingdom, Daniel once again was given a very responsible position.

Daniel was keenly conscious of his personal relationship with God. His wholehearted commitment to Him is reflected in his concern not to defile himself in the idolatrous environs of the royal court in Babylon (ch. 1). This reverence or fear of God is also expressed by Daniel in his courteous attitude toward his superiors during his captivity. Completely divorced from the legalistic or ritualistic observance of the law associated with the temple in Jerusalem, Daniel exemplified a concern for making the heart of the Mosaic revelation—a wholehearted love for God—a practical reality in his daily pattern of living.

Throughout his life Daniel apparently maintained this vital relationship with God. In the crucial experience (ch. 2) when he faced execution, Daniel, together with the companions, prayed for "mercy of the God of Heaven." Subsequently through a divine revelation he was enabled to relate to King Nebuchadnezzar his dream and its interpretation.

This king of Babylon recognized Daniel as a God-fearing person. Daniel had his first opportunity to share his knowledge of God as he reported the dream and its interpretation indicating that ultimately the God of heaven would establish a kingdom without end. Subsequently when Nebuchadnezzar had another dream he turned to Daniel, acknowledging that Daniel had the Spirit of the holy God (ch. 4). Years later when Belshazzar was faced with the mysterious handwriting on the banquet-room wall, Daniel once again was singled out as a man who had

---

167 B.C., see Otto Eissfeldt, *The Old Testament* (New York: Harper & Row, 1965), pp. 512–29.

a vital relationship with God (ch. 5). In response to the king's request he interpreted the sobering announcement of God's judgment.

In the Medo-Persian era, when Daniel had again risen to a top-level administrative position, the character of Daniel emerges once more as that of a God-fearing person. It is apparent that Daniel in his daily life reflected a consciousness of God. After a thorough investigation his political critics found nothing questionable about his ethics and practices in his administrative responsibilities or in his relationship with his fellow men. His standard of morality and pattern of daily living were beyond criticism. No charges of injustice or bribery could be directed against him. The crucial point in which they temporarily succeeded in indicting him was the matter of his wholehearted devotion to God.

Daniel's devotion to God is clearly delineated in 6:10. Prayer seemed to be part of his daily pattern of living as he expressed his thanksgiving to God in an attitude of true worship. The fact that he faced Jerusalem suggests that he had a concern for the future of the Jewish nation. Even though he had personally prospered he had not permitted the endowment of political power and prestige to diminish his love for God and the promises made to his people Israel. It was the reading of Jeremiah that prompted him to intercede earnestly in intercessory prayer for the restoration of Israel (9:1ff.).

To the man Daniel came the unique revelation about the future developments from the international perspective.[2] That a series of kingdoms would rise and fall is repeatedly indicated through Nebuchadnezzar's dream and subsequent divine reve-

[2] For a chronological arrangement of the book of Daniel relating the dreams and visions to the international developments during Daniel's lifetime, see S. J. Schultz, *The Old Testament Speaks* (New York: Harper & Row, 1960), pp. 365–76.

lations to Daniel. Although these provide a general outline of future developments which have been subject to varied interpretations, certain aspects seem to emerge explicitly in the scriptural text and context.

Nebuchadnezzar is identified as the head of gold, indicating that Babylonia is the first of successive kingdoms (2:37). Daniel, in response to his inquiry and concern, is divinely informed that Medo-Persia and Greece will follow as great powers of international might (8:20–26). The latter will be divided into four parts. A God-defiant king will inflict persecution on the saints but his power will be broken by nonhuman might.

Another aspect of this kingdom series is the perspective of an ultimate kingdom that will endure forever (2:44–45; 7:13–14, 18, 21–27). This kingdom will be established through supernatural intervention, since the ruler is identified as the God of heaven or Ancient of Days.[3] Associated with him in this reign are the "saints" or "people of the saints of the Most High." In all likelihood these saints are later identified to Daniel as "your people" (in 9:24 and 12:1–4), referring to the remnant of Israel who are delivered out of great trouble and joined by those who are resurrected to everlasting life.

The total period allotted to Daniel's people is seventy weeks (9:24), usually translated as "seventy weeks of years" making a total of 490 years. These weeks are divided into three periods, consisting of seven weeks or forty-nine years, sixty-two weeks or 434 years, and one week or seven years. The starting point of this seventy-week period is the command to rebuild Jerusalem. The first two periods terminate with the appearance of the Messiah who was subsequently "cut off." The final one

[3] The book by Robert D. Culver, *Daniel and the Latter Days* (Westwood, N.J.: Fleming H. Revell Co., 1954), offers a premillennial interpretation of Daniel. For a commentary projecting an amillennial viewpoint, see E. J. Young, *The Prophecy of Daniel* (Grand Rapids: Eerdmans, 1949).

week, or seven years, seems to be a subsequent period interrupted in the middle by the termination of sacrifice and offering. The fact that the total period for Israel is seventy weeks suggests that this last seven-year period immediately precedes the consummation of all things or the beginning of the everlasting kingdom which was the climax for Daniel's people, as indicated previously.

Unlike Isaiah, the prophetic perspective of Daniel does not include the mission of the suffering servant through whom salvation is extended to the Gentiles. Daniel, primarily viewing developments from the pinnacle of powerful kingdoms, sees through divine revelation the final restoration prospects for his people Israel. Even though his people will be subjected to suffering intensively under God-defiant rulers, these kingdoms will finally be terminated as the everlasting kingdom emerges. Daniel is personally assured that he will stand in his lot at the end of the days.

HAGGAI

Nearly two decades had passed since the exiles returned from Babylon to Jerusalem when Haggai delivered his prophetic messages. Although they had immediately resumed sacrifice and festal activities (Ezra 1–3), their enemies successfully kept them from rebuilding the temple. Consequently they had become absorbed in building fine houses for their own comfort.

Haggai, as a prophet speaking for God, was primarily concerned about their relationship with God. They had become so engrossed with selfish, materialistic interests of building beautiful homes that they lacked motivation to rebuild the Lord's house (1:7). The sacrifices and services they rendered were not pleasing to God because the people themselves were not genuinely devoted to God (2:10–14). Service and sacrifice offered by the people who lacked a wholehearted love for God were not favorable to obtaining God's blessing. Haggai assured them of God's favor and prosperity if they turned their attention to the rebuilding of the temple.

ZECHARIAH

Explicitly Zechariah points out in his introductory message that the temple was reduced to ruins because their forefathers had not listened to the warnings of the prophets. Their rebellious attitude and lack of reverence, respect, and wholehearted love toward God had precipitated this terrible judgment in the destruction of Jerusalem. Maintaining a right relationship with God—this is the lesson the returning exiles ought to learn from history, asserts Zechariah. They ought to repent and not act as their fathers did (1:1–6).

What about future prospects? Since the previous temple was destroyed, what will happen to this one if they succeed in rebuilding it? What about Israel's guilt? What about the long-range hopes of restoration of the kingdom of Israel? In symbolic language Zechariah answers these questions in his second message, based on a series of visions (1:7–6:14). Although much of this passage is obscure the main ideas are more readily apparent.

Presently God, the Lord of Hosts, is returning with mercy and compassion to Jerusalem. The temple will be rebuilt. Prosperity and comfort are in store for Jerusalem and Judah. The world powers that scattered the Israelites will be terminated (1:7–21).

A vast expansion of Jerusalem, extending the population far beyond the city walls, is assured. Even in Nehemiah's time, about seventy years later, such vast areas within the walled boundary of Jerusalem were unoccupied that a conscription was necessary to bring residents from surrounding towns to establish homes in the city so that the wall would be properly guarded (Neh. 11:1–2). Such a population expansion envisioned by Zechariah has not yet been realized even today, since with it the Lord Himself will be the glory of the Holy City of Jerusalem and will provide a wall of fire for protection.

Atonement for Israel's sin was assured in the divine provision qualifying Joshua to sacrifice so that Israel could be restored to a right relationship with God. With this came the promise of God's future provision in his servant, the branch through whom the sin of Israel would be removed in a single day. After this, absolute peace and prosperity will prevail so that everyone with his neighbor will dwell in security (3:1–10).

The Lord's continual everlasting watchfulness over Israel is vividly portrayed in the automatic unending supply of oil for the golden seven-lipped lampstand furnished by two olive trees. The latter represented the two anointed ones who assist the Lord whose eyes see everywhere throughout the whole earth (4:1–14).

Although the flying scroll explicitly stated Israel's guilt in transgression, comfort came in the realization that the iniquity of Israel was transported to the land of Shinar, or Babylon (5:1–11). With the chariots patrolling the whole earth and the crowning of Joshua, the audience of Zechariah is again offered assurance that the Lord of Hosts is in control. Through their obedience to Him they can proceed in confidence as they rebuild the temple of God.

When the question of the traditional fast was raised two years later, Zechariah pointedly elaborated on the basic problem of Israel's relationship with God. Fasting for the sake of fasting was futile. Observance of feasts and perfunctory performances of rituals were useless in an attitude of self-interest instead of wholehearted devotion to God. Wrath and divine judgment had come to their forefathers because they failed in demonstrating justice and love toward their fellow men, even ignoring the warnings given through the prophets (7:1–14).

By contrast to the destroyed city which in his day was partially occupied, Zechariah assures this small discouraged remnant of the ultimate peace and prosperity awaiting Jerusalem (8:1–23). Israelites will be gathered from the east and from the west. Jerusalem will be known as the "faithful city and the mountain of the Lord of hosts, the holy mountain." So evident will the divine blessing be in Jerusalem that nations and individuals will curry the favor of the Jews to seek the Lord of Hosts. With these words Zechariah encouraged the generation in which he was living to continue diligently in the building of the temple that had previously been razed in judgment because of the sins of their forefathers.

In typical prophetic language, Zechariah projects in the final part of his book the conditions related to the establishment of the ultimate kingdom. Although numerous aspects of these unfolding plans seem ambiguous, certain features emerge as various parts of this message are integrated.

Jerusalem is crucially important in these final developments. Nations who become involved with the city of Jerusalem will find it to be a burdensome stone or a cup of poison to their own destruction or ruination (12:2–3). The Lord will protect Jerusalem, seeking to destroy all nations that declare war against it (12:8). The residents of Jerusalem will be endued with a spirit of compassion and prayer so that they will recognize "Him whom they have pierced" (12:10). Security and holiness will prevail throughout the city of Jerusalem (14:11, 20–21). From the city of Jerusalem will issue streams of living water (14:8).

Israel will be regathered from distant lands even as a shepherd gathers his sheep (10:8–12). Non-Israelites who intermarry with them will worship the true God instead of the Israelites' turning to the idols of surrounding nations (9:1–8). Israel will be refined by fire, suffering in the conflict and losing about two-thirds of its population. The remnant, or remaining third, will genuinely acknowledge God. Cleansing from iniquity will be provided for Israel so that idolatry, false prophets, and deceivers will be totally removed from the land (13:1–9). They will acknowledge and rejoice in the Lord as their God (13:1–9).

Other nations will challenge Israel's regathering and will mobilize against Jerusalem (14:1–6), but God will intervene for Israel. Enemies will be blinded (12:4) and panic-stricken, so that their wealth will be confiscated (14:12–15). Rain will be withheld from all who refuse to worship God.

God's covenant with Israel has not been forgotten. Israel's deliverance comes because of God's covenant (9:11–17). The restoration of Israel was a manifestation of God's compassion and love extended to them (10:6).

The King of Zion is portrayed as one who is victorious and triumphant yet humble and riding upon an ass (9:9). Although this aspect of his humble appearance was realized in the triumphal entry of Jesus into Jerusalem, the establishment of a worldwide dominion when He will speak peace to the nations awaits fulfillment (9:10). As King, the Lord will appear on the Mount of Olives, dividing it from east to west to fight against the nations gathered against Jerusalem (14:1–8). In a continuous day, or unending period, the Lord will become King over all the earth. The survivors of all nations will worship the Lord of Hosts and participate in the sacred festivities. In this manner the ultimate kingdom will be established with the Israelites enjoying absolute peace and prosperity in their own land.

MALACHI

In a concise and pointed message Malachi speaks directly to the issue of man's relationship with God. He indicts his audience for not responding to God's love and mistreating their fellow men. For ignoring this law of love they will be judged by God. Individual accountability is certain, since God will divide the righteous and the wicked for reward and punishment. Before that day of ultimate judgment God will send His Messenger, providing another opportunity to repent.

"I have loved you," says Malachi, speaking for God. This points back to the heart of the covenant relationship established under Moses. God is the Great King (1:14). The day is coming when He will be greatly revered by all Gentiles and yet the Israelites now fail to revere and honor Him. Their lives reflected failure on their part to respond with love, reverence, and honor in their attitude toward God.

The priests or religious leaders bear the greatest guilt. They offered polluted sacrifices and were guilty of advising people that they could bring lame animals for sacrifice when they knew that God required the very best. At the same time they recited a prayer for God's mercy. How could they expect God to favor them when such hypocrisy prevailed? A father would not tolerate such treatment by his son, nor a master by his servant. How did they dare to treat God in this way? Hardly a priest could be found who would have the courage to act in accordance with God's instructions and refuse such sacrifices because they were dishonoring to God.

In the future God's name will be revered among the Gentile nations continually. The time is coming when they will offer sweet incense and bring pure, acceptable offerings genuinely honoring to God. At present the Israelites who are God's covenant people dare to bring sick animals as offerings when they appear before Him in worship. They would not think of treating their governor with such a lack of respect. They would not dare to ignore his requirements or desires in their concern to serve him. Consequently it is high time that God's people examine their relationship with God their King.

The purpose of God's covenant is clearly stated—to give life and peace (2:5–9). Moses had already asserted this when he expounded the terms of God's covenant to the generation that was about to enter and occupy Canaan (Deut. 31:1–13). The religious leaders were responsible to teach the people fear and respect for God by carefully observing what God required of them—a wholehearted love for God—in response to his love for them. Genuine love in daily life would involve a careful consideration of what God expected in sacrifice and offerings. Religious leaders who heeded the divine instructions lived a good and righteous life, and by precept and example caused others to do the same thing. It is the priest who is responsible for informing the layman what the Lord of Hosts has prescribed in the law. Unfortunately the priests were showing partiality in interpreting and administering the law—for this they would be judged.

The basic problem was not one of legalism. Their attitude toward God was not right (2:10–17). Their theology was correct or orthodox in recognizing that God had created each one of them. However, they seemed to blame God for the fact that they were mistreating each other, failing to show love for one another. While partial in their teaching of the law, profaning the sanctuary, accepting inferior offerings, weeping and groaning or complaining at the altar because their offerings were not accepted, the leaders assure the people that God delights in their pattern of living and naïvely ask, "Where is the God of justice or judgment?"

A God-sent messenger is promised (3:1–5). This one will

come for a twofold purpose. He will refine and purify people so that acceptable offerings will once again be offered. He will also come to judge. Justice will be meted out to those who have mistreated their fellow men. God's mercy will be terminated for those who, instead of loving their neighbors, trick the innocent, commit adultery, lie, cheat the wage-earner, take advantage of widows and orphans, turn aside the foreigners or strangers, and fail to revere or fear God. All these evil deeds, concerning which there was ample warning in the Mosaic revelation, cannot be overlooked by God their King.

Having delineated their failure to exercise the law of love toward one another—love your neighbor as yourself—Malachi directs or reverts his message again to the basic problem: failure to love and revere God (3:6–15). God's day of judgment is certain, but this day is not dated. Presently God's mercy is still extended, providing opportunity for them to repent and confess their sin. Their failure to acknowledge their sin toward God brings into consideration another indictment that can be definitely identified: they have robbed God by not giving Him a tenth of their income. Pride and arrogance however are at the basis of their failure to acknowledge God.

The law of love is definitely applied as Malachi speaks of the final judgment. The basis for divine judgment of men is vividly delineated. The Great King who extended His love and mercy in His covenant treaty with Israel will execute judgment for each individual on the basis of his personal response to God's love (3:16–4:6). Those who love God, respecting and revering Him so that they have applied the instructions divinely revealed through Moses concerning their relationship to their fellow men, will be spared by God in the day of judgment. They have their names recorded in God's book of remembrance. Upon them God's mercy will continue without end.

The arrogant, the proud, those who have ignored or failed to respond to God's love for them so that they have spurned God's instructions concerning neighborly love, those who have considered it foolish to worship God, or have been unwilling to confess their sin—these face the day of judgment before the Great King. For them the day of judgment is coming like a burning furnace.

Malachi, like Moses and the other prophets, points to the basic responsibility of man to love and revere God. A genuine love for God should also be reflected in this relationship with his fellow men. For these there is the promise of God's everlasting mercy. Likewise Malachi agrees with the prophets before him that those who don't love and respect God await the day of God's judgment and curse.

Malachi's message concludes with hope for his generation. Before that dreadful day of judgment God is sending His messenger to turn people Godward. Mercy precedes God's final judgment. God's love still prevails.

X

THE PROPHET SPEAKS

FOUR centuries passed without the voice of a prophet. The promise of the last prophet, Malachi, had offered hope that God would send some one likened to Elijah. Passages such as II Macc. 2:46 and others reflect the anticipation of the fulfillment of this prophetic promise. Individuals like Simeon and Anna (Luke 2) may have been representative of many devout people who prayerfully lived in the hope of seeing the God-sent messenger.

RELIGION IN NEW TESTAMENT TIMES

An intensive concern for keeping the law was a distinctive mark of postexilic religion in Israel. Throughout the centuries of political tensions, as Persian domination gave way to Greek and Roman supremacy, bringing changing cultures and fortunes to bear upon the Jews, the pattern of living prescribed for God's holy people became the focal point of interest.

As the study of the law increased, disciples gathered around teachers such as Ben Sira (Ecclus. 38:24–34; 51:23). Very likely he belonged to the professional scribes and may have conducted an academy in Jerusalem where he lectured to youth on ethical and religious subjects.[1] In the course of time many of the com-

[1] Cf. Bruce Metzger, *An Introduction to the Apocrypha* (New York: Oxford University Press, 1957), p. 78.

mands in the law were given detailed definitions and interpretations (Jubilee 50:1–13). By way of example, the Sabbath law could be suspended for defense purposes (I Macc. 2:29–41). In this way a hedge was built around the law (P. Aboth 1:1) as adjustment was made to the changing situations in varied circumstances.

For many generations these interpretations were transmitted orally and became known as oral laws. Sects such as the Sadducees and the Pharisees developed, reflecting varied views of interpretation. The latter advocated minute observance of the law and made the oral law obligatory, while the former accepted only the Torah. By about A.D. 200 these oral laws were codified in the Mishnah and later completed in the Talmud. Although the list of 613 laws was completed in medieval times by Maimonides it is generally held that the broad outlines of these were part of the oral tradition of first-century Judaism.

Regardless of sect, however, basic in the religion of the Jews was the concern to fulfill the requirements of the written law. The sum of all righteousness was to keep the law. Consequently Judaism was constantly facing the danger of legalism or of becoming a religion in which a man's works determined his status before God. This externalizing of righteousness was seemingly never checked in Judaism in subsequent centuries.

The moral and ethical teachings in the synagogue during the middle forty years of the first century of the Christian Era are best known to us through the Gospels.[2] Jesus in His ministry of teaching and healing constantly mingled with all classes of society from publicans and sinners to the most righteous among the religious leaders. Numerous dialogues between Jesus and Pharisees, Sadducees, and scribes provide insight into the re-

[2] George Foot Moore, *Judaism in the First Centuries of the Christian Era* (Cambridge, Mass.: Harvard University Press, 1927–1930), Vol. I, p. 132.

ligious climate during that generation. Added to these are the discourses of Jesus and that which He taught by way of example.

The extensive legalistic externalism reflected in the Mishnah and later in the Talmud should not be regarded as the norm for Judaism in the days of Jesus.[3] Pharisaistic piety is definitely portrayed as being primarily formalistic or external. John the Baptist referred to the Pharisees, as well as the Sadducees and the multitude (Matt. 3:7ff.; Luke 3:7ff.), as a "generation of vipers" as far as their relationship with God was concerned. Jesus disclosed their hearts as being evil while they pretended to exhibit good outward deeds (Matt. 12:33–37). In His teaching, Jesus described the external righteousness of the Pharisees but indicated that a higher standard was necessary to enter the kingdom (Matt. 5:20–6:18; Luke 11:42). Jesus' incisive observation was that they honored God with their lips but their hearts were far removed from Him (Matt. 7:1–20; Mark 7:1–23). In His indictment of the scribes and the Pharisees, He identified them as hypocrites.

Josephus likewise points to external piety when he reports that a certain Pharisee named Ananias observed the religious fast for the purpose of achieving his political goals. Furthermore, sacred festivals were often observed by Jewish leaders for political advantages. Seditions were frequently initiated during these religious observances. According to Josephus, such formalistic piety was an accepted standard for many Jews.[4]

The fact that external piety so extensively permeated Judaism

[3] In the Mishnah, which was codified between A.D. 200–600, the short passages in the Pentateuch concerning the Sabbath are expanded to 39 articles and 1,521 passages according to P. P. Bläser, *Das Gesetz bei Paulus* (Münster: Aschendorff, 1941), p. 39. R. H. Longenecker, *Paul Apostle of Liberty* (New York: Harper & Row, 1964), pp. 67–68, points out that here is "a pitifully small amount of direct Talmudic evidence" going back to the predestruction period before A.D. 70, and that very few sayings ascribed to antiquity emphasize mere externalism.

[4] Josephus, *Life,* 56.

during the time of Jesus should not obscure the fact that there were individuals who reflected true genuine religion. Mechanical conformity to the law was never the aim or objective of the most devout teachers. Hillel and some of the other Jewish teachers of that era are quoted in the early Jewish writings as emphasizing the fact that the external rites and actions in themselves are not meritorious and that a good heart is the source of all good. Significant is the fact that in the Shema, which was recited daily by the Jews in this early period, the matter of obedience came third in order after a confession or affirmation of the unity of God and man. This order was also followed in the Shemoneh Esreh (the Eighteen "Benedictions") and the 613 commandments.[5] The service of man came in order after the acknowledgment of God and of a wholehearted love for Him. Through these the Talmudic emphasis of the love of God as the proper motivation for living the religious life seems to reflect the concern of the best teachers in Jewish history even before A.D. 70 when the temple was destroyed.

The Gospels as well as Josephus also bear witness that there were some religious leaders who had the Mosaic perspective of what was important in man's relationship with God. Jesus spoke favorably of one scribe who recognized that love for God and man had priority over ritualism and service (Mark 12:28–34). Consider also Nicodemus (John 3:1; 19:39), Joseph of Arimathea (Mark 15:43), and other Pharisees who were favorably disposed toward Jesus and His teaching (Luke 13:31; 14:1). Josephus reports that Alexander Jannaeus considered most of the Pharisees scoundrels but did recognize a godly element among them.[6]

[5] Cf. *The Jewish Encyclopedia,* Vol. IV, pp. 181–186, in the article "The 613 Commandments" by I. Broyde, concerning the listing and antiquity of these commandments.

[6] Cf. Longenecker, *op. cit.,* pp. 70–74, for a discussion of the righteous

Although the religious climate into which Jesus came seemed to be predominantly legalistic there were those who had a sense of true righteousness. The concept of a genuine mutual love relationship between man and God and the consideration for one's fellow men was still preserved by some of the leading teachers and by a minority of God-fearing people even among the Pharisees.

JESUS THE PROPHET

Jesus was recognized as a prophet by the generation in which He lived. Philip, after meeting Jesus, identified Him to Nathanael as the one "of whom Moses and the prophets did write" (John 1:45). The teaching and healing ministry of Jesus brought the popular response or acclaim from the people throughout Galilee, Judea including Jerusalem, and Samaria that God had visited His people Israel in sending them a prophet (Luke 7:16, 39; John 4:19; 7:40; and other references). The consensus seemed to be that Jesus was John the Baptist, Elijah, Jeremiah, or one of the prophets (Matt. 16:14; 21:46). Nicodemus, a ruler among the Pharisees, represented those who recognized Jesus as "a teacher come from God" (John 3:2). Frequently Jesus was regarded as a teacher with a school of disciples.[7] Jesus, as is reported by all four Gospels, spoke of Himself as a prophet. The preaching of the kingdom of God, a subject so prominent in many of the prophets, was a stated purpose of His life (Luke 4:43).

Jesus was in harmony with the prophets before Him. Not only did He agree with the written revelation given through

---

element in Judaism in the predestruction period. Also see A. Lukyn Williams, *Talmudic Judaism and Christianity* (London: S.P.C.K., 1933), pp. 38–43, for the theology of the Palestinian Pharisees before A.D. 70.

[7] Note the titles applied to Jesus during His ministry: *Didaskale* in John 11:28; 13:13–14; Matt. 8:19; Mark 4:38; *Epistata* in Luke 5:5; 8:24, 45; 9:33, 49; 17:13; *Rabbi* in John 1:38, 49; 3:2; 3:26; 6:25; *Rabbouni* in John 20:16.

Moses and the prophets, but He definitely stated that He had come to fulfill the law and the prophets (Matt. 5:17). As a teacher Jesus taught and participated in the services of the synagogues throughout the land of Palestine. In keeping with the belief common among the Jews, Jesus accepted the Scriptures as authoritative and as the basis of appeal for all matters pertaining to religion. There is no evidence pointing to any difference of opinion between Jesus and the religious leaders of that day concerning the extent of literature accepted as inspired, namely the twenty-two books of the Jewish canon commonly identified as "the Law and the Prophets" in the New Testament writings.[8]

MORE THAN A PROPHET

Although Jesus came in the succession of prophets, He boldly asserted that He was more than a spokesman for God. This distinction is clearly apparent throughout His teaching ministry. Whereas the prophets repeatedly prefaced their messages with "thus saith the Lord," and the contemporary teachers appealed to the law and the prophets in their teaching, Jesus taught on an authority "from heaven" (John 3:13) beyond His appeal to the Scriptures. Although the religious leaders challenged Him on His authority they were not successful in counteracting Him as a teacher of the populace (Matt. 21:23–27; Mark 11:27–33; Luke

[8] The literature contained in the twenty-two books of the Hebrew Canon is identical with the thirty-nine books in the English Bible. Throughout the New Testament the Hebrew Canon is repeatedly identified as "the law and the prophets." Cf. Acts 24:14 where Paul and his accusers obviously agreed on the extent of the canon under this title. The threefold division, law—5, prophets—8, and hagiographa—11, developed after the New Testament era. Josephus referred to twenty-two books, with law—5, prophets—13, and other books—4. Whether this was a standard division or his own classification is uncertain. Since this literature was kept on scrolls the order varied. When the codex or book form replaced the scroll in the second century of the Christian Era an order or arrangement became necessary.

20:1–8; John 7:40–53). Jesus was not ordained as a rabbi but gave proper recognition to the authority of rabbinic succession.[9] In the confusion prevailing in a religious climate permeated by tradition and legalism, Jesus astonished the crowds with the unique distinction that "he taught them as one having authority and not as the scribes" (Matt. 7:28).

Unlike the prophets, Jesus boldly claimed that He was one with God, His Father. Peter and others confessed that He was the Son of God (Matt. 16:16, and other passages). Christ's claim to divinity became an issue so disturbing to the religious leaders of His day that after numerous crises it led to His trial and death. When, at the time of Christ's triumphal entry into Jerusalem, the multitude addressed to Jesus the prayer in Ps. 118:25, which was directed to God by the psalmist, the religious leaders were enraged. Unable to control the multitude, the Pharisees appealed to Jesus to rebuke His disciples and the children. By this desperate appeal the critics directly confronted Jesus with His claim to be equal with God and on that basis accepting prayer and praise which the psalmist had addressed to God. No prophet before, apostle later, ever allowed himself such acclaim. Instead of pacifying His critics, Jesus Christ rebuked them with the words of the psalmist, "Out of the mouth of babes and sucklings thou hast perfected praise" (Matt. 21:1–17; Luke 19:28–40).

Unlike the prophets before Him, Jesus accepted worship. When He identified Himself as the Son of God to the blind man whose sight had been restored, Jesus accepted his response in faith and worship (John 9:35–38). Other individuals who worshipped Jesus were the leper (Matt. 8:2), a certain ruler (Matt. 9:18), and the woman of Canaan (Matt. 15:25).

[9] Cf. Longenecker, *op. cit.,* p. 140. For a correlation of the two elements —the formalistic and the inward spirit within predestruction Hebraic Pharisaism—see pp. 74–79.

Jesus asserted that He was the manifestation of God Himself (John 14:7–12). No prophet, not even Moses, ever said, "I am the way, the truth, and the life" or "I am the light of the world" or "I am the bread of life." Unprecedented was the claim "I am the resurrection and the life" and unique was the resurrection of Jesus Christ to confirm this claim, as is evident in the messages of the apostles in the book of Acts.[10]

FULFILLMENT OF THE LAW

Jesus came to fulfill the law and the prophets—not to abolish them. The crucial passage (Matt. 5:17–20) deserves careful consideration as it relates to the Scriptures, the cultural and religious context, and the mission of Jesus.

Frequently this statement by Jesus has been interpreted as referring only to the law of Moses. Jesus, however, specifically says the *law* and the *prophets*—a descriptive reference used repeatedly in the New Testament to identify that body of literature which the Jews regarded as inspired and which was in the Christian Era and is today commonly called the Old Testament.

Although the word "law" in Matt. 5:18 could be interpreted in a restricted sense it is likewise possible that Jesus here referred to the entire Old Testament. Such seems to be the case in John 10:34 where Jesus quotes from Ps. 82 and reminds his listeners that this is written in their law. This may also be the meaning of the term "law" in Luke 16:17 where it could represent the entire Jewish canon.

The Scriptures were regarded by the Jews as the expression of God's will. They represented the written revelation of what

[10] Ethelbert Stauffer asserts that Jesus, in using the Old Testament and liturgical theophanic formula *Ani hu* or "I am He," meant to "convey that in his life the historical epiphany of God was taking place," and that this expression was "the purest, the boldest, and the profoundest declaration by Jesus of who and what he was" (cf. *Jesus and His Story,* tr. by Richard and Clara Winston [New York: Alfred A. Knopf, 1960], pp. 174–95).

God wanted His people to know as He had revealed it through Moses and the prophets. The divine revelation through Moses established Israel as a nation, as recorded in Exodus through Deuteronomy. The essential background and introduction is given in Genesis where God's relationship to the entire human race and the patriarchs is unfolded. The historical account and the messages of the prophets were considered an essential part of the Scriptures as they provided supplementary information to the Mosaic revelation as it was given through the prophets. In "Moses and all the prophets" much had been written concerning the promises of God and the restoration of the kingdom.

Jesus came to fulfill the Scriptures. Without question He penetrated the multitude of conflicting interpretations of the Law which were so well known to that generation, and spoke with authority concerning the true meaning and interpretation of God's will. It was necessary to cut through the casuistry and legalism associated with the observance of the law. This, however, should not obscure the broader scope of Jesus' statement in asserting that He came to fulfill the law and the prophets.

How did Jesus approach the problem of fulfilling the requirements of the law and the prophets which Judaism considered the basis to faith and practice? In a dialogue with His severest critics when He was questioned by a lawyer of the Pharisees, Jesus made several observations which are crucial to this issue. Without the dispute of His critics, Jesus pointed to the two requirements which represented the heart of the law, namely, genuine love for God and for one's neighbor. Jesus added the significant observation that everything in the law and the prophets depended upon these requirements (Matt. 22:34–40). To the scribe who recognized these as more important than the external conformity to the law in bringing offerings and sacrifices, Jesus gave the assuring words, "Thou art not far from the kingdom of God" (Mark 12:28–34). The lawyer, who may have participated in this same discussion and posed the question, "What shall I do to inherit eternal life?" observed that the essential requirements of the law were to love God and to love one's neighbor as oneself. Concurring with the lawyer, Jesus assured him of eternal life (Luke 10:25–28).

There is no indication that Jesus held that the legalistic observance of the Mosaic law assured an individual of eternal life and righteousness before God. Under crucial cross examination Jesus and the contemporary religious leaders agreed that the law primarily pointed to a right relationship with God and man rather than to the legalistic observance of its details. This interpretation was confirmed by subsequent prophets and finally by Jesus Himself.

Cutting through the prevailing fabric of religious externalism, Jesus through precept and example projected a proper perspective toward that which had been revealed in the law and the prophets. Those who adhere to legalism or an outward standard of observing the law without a right relationship with God were denounced by Jesus in no uncertain terms. At the same time He did not abrogate practical righteousness but asserted that those who would enter the kingdom of heaven must have a righteousness that exceeds that of the scribes and the Pharisees (Matt. 5:20; cf. also Luke 11:42). In His teaching, Jesus gave new commandments and indicated that conformity to His teaching would be genuine proof of a wholehearted love toward God. Amid the confusion of so many interpretations orally known to that generation He authoritatively pointed out what was correct.[11] Sensitive to the casuistry and externalism exhibited in keeping the law, Jesus pointed to its true meaning as given to Israel through Moses.

Repeatedly Jesus asserted that He had come to fulfill the

[11] Cf. D. Daube, *The New Testament and Rabbinic Judaism* (London: Athlone Press, 1956), pp. 55–62.

Scriptures (Matt. 3:15; 5:17; 26:54; Mark 1:15; 14:49; Luke 4:21; 24:44). In the apostolic preaching and teaching in the early church as portrayed in the book of Acts, testimony is often given to the recognition that Jesus had come in fulfillment of Old Testament prophecies. The way in which Jesus fulfilled the two basic requirements of the law needs consideration in the light of His life and teaching.

Jesus Christ in His incarnation represented the unique manifestation of God's love to man. Even though love and mercy were continually extended to all mankind by God in sending rain and sunshine upon the just and the unjust (Matt. 5:45), it was God's gift in sending His only Son that revealed His love for the human race (John 3:16; 17:23). The apostle Paul recognized Jesus as the expression of God's love for man (Rom. 5:8; cf. also I John 4:9).

Unfolding God's love for the human race, Jesus Christ through His life, teaching, death, and resurrection demonstrated and fulfilled that perfect commitment of love to God and fellow men in which the Israelites had failed. God had bestowed His love upon Israel (Deut. 10:12–22) with the intent that they should extend this love to their neighbors. As God's servant, Israel had failed in this mission so that God sent His only Son as the "righteous servant" to fulfill the divine plan to reach all mankind. In this manner Jesus fulfilled the mission of God's servant as delineated in Isa. 41:8–53:12.

Throughout His life Jesus exemplified a wholehearted love and devotion to God. To Mary His mother, who found Him in the temple, Jesus replied that His foremost concern was to be in His Father's house (Luke 2:49). Frequently He withdrew from the multitude and even from His disciples in order to pray and commune with God (Matt. 14:23; Mark 1:35; Luke 5:16). To His disciples, Jesus frankly stated that doing God's will was more important to Him than food for His body (John

4:34). When wrestling with suffering and death in Gethsemane, Jesus agonized in prayer, saying, "Not my will but thine" as He communed with God (Matt. 26:36–46; Mark 14:32–43; Luke 22:39–46). Near the end of His earthly ministry, Jesus affirmed that He had kept His Father's commandments (John 15:10).

Jesus came for the express purpose of ministering to others. He taught that love and mercy should be extended not only to those who reciprocate but to the enemy as well (Matt. 5:39–48; Luke 6:27–36; cf. also Rom. 12:20). This Godlike trait of manifesting love and mercy to the ungrateful and selfish should be characteristic of those who were sons of God. Even as Moses admonished the Israelites to love the stranger because they had been loved by God when they were strangers in Egypt (Deut. 10:19–22), so Jesus points out that those who have been recipients of God's mercy should be merciful even as God is merciful. To the lawyer who in self-justification asked, "And who is my neighbor?" Jesus gave the example of the Samaritan who out of a heart of compassion rendered social service where it was needed (Luke 10:29–37).

While Jesus lived within the framework of the written law, or Torah, He disregarded the Pharisaic principle of separation in associating with and accepting the hospitality of publicans and sinners, running the risk of ceremonial defilement (Mark 2:16; Luke 15:2; 19:7).[12] Although severely criticized, Jesus ministered to Zaccheus, to the Samaritans, to the sinful woman who anointed Him, and to others. By allowing His disciples to pluck grain and by performing acts of healing on the Sabbath, He ignored and defied the Pharisaic restrictions and taught that the Sabbath was made for man and not man for the Sabbath (Mark 2:15–3:6). In this manner Jesus very definitely empha-

[12] Cf. B. H. Branscomb, *Jesus and the Law of Moses* (London: Hodder and Stoughton, 1930), p. 135, and Daube, *op. cit.*, pp. 373–74. For a discussion of "Christ and the Law," see Longenecker, *op. cit.*, pp. 136ff.

sized the priority of the two basic requirements of the Scriptures over the legalism that represented the outward adornment of the religious life in that generation.

Incisive and direct is Jesus' analysis of their religion when scribes and Pharisees of Jerusalem raise the issue of the disciples transgressing the traditions of the elders (Matt. 15:1–21). He boldly points out that through their traditions they have nullified the basic commandment of God. True religion begins in the heart and is not primarily judged by the outward appearance. By quoting Isa. 29:13, Jesus identifies the heart as being far from God. When the heart, which should be the source of wholehearted love for God, is the seat of evil and defilement, then the external rites and observances fade into insignificance. Worship of God is hypocritical when human commands are taught as doctrine. In this critical evaluation Jesus taught the true meaning of God's written revelation, negating the religious framework of legalism projected through their traditions.

Jesus went beyond the requirements of the law in deliberately laying down His life (John 10:7–18). This sacrifice was the fulfillment of God's particular command to Him. In this act Jesus demonstrated the "greater love" which was unprecedented in the religion of Israel (John 15:13). Through His voluntary death He exemplified His wholehearted commitment to God in obeying His commandments, thereby manifesting God's love in its fullness to man. Out of this context came the New Commandment.

THE NEW COMMANDMENT

"A new commandment I give unto you that ye love one another; as I have loved, that ye also love one another" (John 13:34; cf. also John 15:12, 17).

In the context of His teaching and personal example, Jesus issued this commandment which was new yet old. Love, which was the key to a right relationship with God and man as revealed through Moses and the prophets, is to continue to be the central core of man's religion. Spoken by Jesus, who was the manifestation of God's love in the form of man, this commandment to love took on a new dimension. This expression of God's love demonstrated through Jesus Christ was to be extended to the entire human race. Whereas Israel had failed as God's servant to accomplish this worldwide mission (Isaiah 40–50), now through the suffering servant and His followers God's love was to be manifested to everyone.

The basic prerequisite for exercising this love is to be responsive to God's love as it is exhibited in Jesus. No one in the human race had had the capacity to respond to God's love as Jesus did while He lived in this world. Having experienced God's love Himself, Jesus demonstrated this love to mankind, as He asserts in John 15:9, "As the father hath loved me so have I loved you." As He responded to God's love so must man respond to Jesus' love in order to be enabled or qualified to love others. Out of the experience and realization of being loved comes the capacity to love others. This provides the basic motivation of true love.

Faith in Jesus Christ as the Son of God is another prerequsite for fulfilling this commandment to love one another. God's love is extended through Christ to everyone who acknowledges "that Jesus came out from God" (John 16:27; cf. also John 17:8). God so loved that He sent His only Son that everyone who believes on Him shall have eternal life. Consequently, response to God's love involves the recognition that Jesus is divine and is truly the Son of God.

The direction of this love is indicated: "that ye love one another." Jesus was concerned that His disciples or those who followed Him should manifest this love to one another. A mutual love relationship was to be the distinctive mark of discipleship (John 13:34). All who love Jesus Christ as the Son of God are enjoined by Him to love one another. This fellowship of those who had a proper relationship with God was already characteristic in Old Testament times, as is expressed by Malachi (3:16–4:6).

The quality of this love is projected with clarity in the words "as I have loved you." It is in the life and teaching of Jesus that this true love is defined and exemplified. Jesus' followers were not left to the changing standards of time and culture but were given a specific directive concerning the nature and quality of this love. Consequently the standard and expression of love must constantly be evaluated on the basis of what Jesus did and taught. Jesus Christ expects His followers to demonstrate the kind of love that He himself projected.

LOVE AND COMMANDMENTS

Genuine love involves keeping the commandments of Jesus. Speaking to His disciples, Jesus pointedly observed, "If a man love me, he will keep my words" (John 14:23; cf. also John 14:15, 21). He makes a marked distinction between those who love Him and those who don't by saying, "He that loveth me not keepeth not my sayings" (John 14:24). A genuine desire to incorporate the teachings and sayings of Jesus Christ in the pattern of everyday living is characteristic of those who wholeheartedly love Him.

Keeping the commandments is the normal result of a love relationship. The corollary to love was obedience in God's covenant with Israel (Deut. 7:9–12). God's mercy was assured those who loved Him and His wrath was upon those who hated Him. In a similar manner Jesus in His teaching points out that the normal sequence issuing out of a love relationship is obedience to the commandments. Love does not issue out of obedience but obedience out of love. The observance of the commandments without the basic love relationship results in legalism—whether it is in reference to the law of Moses in the Old Testament or to the commandments of Jesus in the New Testament.

Commandments are not binding because they are laws. In a relationship of mutual love they provide the knowledge of God's will and the opportunity of pleasing Him in the pattern of daily life. Consequently the principles and moral responsibilities revealed in the written Word of God become important to the one who professes a wholehearted devotion to and love for God.

The commandments and instructions given in the Scriptures are not complete in the sense that they provide the specific course of action in every situation. Basic principles, however, are given which cannot be ignored by those who profess to love Jesus Christ, if this love relationship is to be maintained.

LOVE ETHICS

Augustine, asserting that love is the source principle or core of Christian virtues, reduced the whole Christian ethic to the single maxim: Love, and then what you will, do.[13] This—according to divine revelation given through Moses and the prophets and culminating in the life and teaching of Jesus—is the fountain out of which should issue all of man's actions and behavior. However, the scriptural teaching offers guidance concerning man's involvement in making love the dominating virtue in his total pattern of behavior.

Should decisions be made situationally or prescriptively? Tension between the legalistic and the existential in decision-making can best be resolved by a careful consideration of the fuller teaching on love as given by Jesus. Practical love, which Kant[14]

[13] Augustine, *Ep. Joan.* VII. 5.

[14] Immanuel Kant, *Critique of Practical Reason,* tr. by T. K. Abbott (London: Macmillan & Co., 1923), p. 176.

identified correctly as the "pith of all laws," must find expression in life situations where decisions must be made. Should decisions be controlled by the id (libertinism which is sheer subjectivity and infantilism) or by the superego (legalism which is heteronomy) or by the ego (situationalism which is self-control, autonomous and acting by the "reality principle")?[15]

Jesus recognized these tendencies in man's behavior. Consequently His teaching on love provided the framework in which man's behavioral pattern of self-control could operate with ultimate responsibility and accountability to God. Decisions should then be made in the total situation where the directives, given through divine revelation, are evaluated and considered.

Response—which H. Richard Niebuhr[16] identifies as the key to responsibility—by man should be both vertical toward God and horizontal toward men. Response to the love of God should place man in a situation in which he has the responsibility to emulate the characteristics of God, His Father. Jesus pointed out that man becomes a son of God by responding to His love so that "whosoever believes in him should not perish but have eternal life" (John 3:16–21). As a son of God, having responded to His love, the Christian is to emulate God in attitude and behavior. The character and action of God is the foundation for the Christian ethic (Matt. 5:44–45; Luke 6:27–28, 35–36).[17] God extends His love and mercy to all mankind—the evil and the good, the just and the unjust. Thus the man who has responded Godward in acknowledging divine goodness and mercy should express in Godlike manner his love and goodness to his neighbor—even though that neighbor may not be a friend

[15] See Joseph Fletcher, *Moral Responsibility* (Philadelphia: The Westminster Press, 1967), pp. 237–38.

[16] H. Richard Niebuhr, *The Responsible Self* (New York: Harper & Row, 1963). For further discussion see Niebuhr, *op. cit.*, pp. 231ff.

[17] For discussion see John Murray, *Principles of Conduct* (Grand Rapids: Eerdmans, 1957), pp. 176–80.

but an enemy. To love the enemy seemed to be a "radical obligation of the Christian ethic"[18] when Jesus said it in the context of Pharisaic tradition, even as it is in modern times. God's attitude in expressing a concern for all mankind—showing mercy to the ungrateful and selfish, to the just and the unjust (Luke 6:35), and by sending His son into the world that man might respond and eternally enjoy divine favor (John 3:16–19)—is to be reflected in man's behavior in love for his neighbor.

Although decisions must be made in the situation in relationship with his neighbor, the moral responsibility rests on man to emulate God as He is revealed through the prophets and through Jesus Christ. The law of love serves as a guiding framework in which the ego exercises an intelligent control reflecting God's love. In this manner the ego or superego does not function for the love of the law but serves the law of love as projected by Jesus.

Right and wrong depend upon the total situation. The responsible individual devoted in love to God faces these decisions with the background of the knowledge of Him and the love and compassion he should exercise as a son of God.

JESUS AND THE KINGDOM

Jesus, like the prophets before Him, announced the restoration of the kingdom. Paradoxically He spoke of the kingdom "within you" and the kingdom "to come." Throughout His teaching ministry He delineated the characteristics of those who would ultimately share in the kingdom of God and those who would not enter the kingdom.

The law of love was the means of identifying those who would finally share in God's kingdom, which Jesus equated with eternal life. In the Mosaic revelation those who responded to God's love with a commitment that issued in obedience were

[18] Cf. Fletcher, *op. cit.,* p. 21.

assured of His favor and blessing. Those who ignored God and spurned His lovingkindness were warned of His curse and judgment to come. Moses delineated the way of "life and good, death and evil" (Deut. 30:15). Prophet after prophet warned people of judgment because of their disobedience but hopefully assured those who responded in love and obedience that the kingdom would be restored.

Jesus likewise emphasized the love and justice of God. Central in His teaching was the message of God's love and mercy extended to all mankind, but He did not omit the corollary of God's righteousness and justice which would follow the day of His love and mercy. Jesus warned His generation that Jerusalem would be destroyed because they had rejected the prophets and their messages (Matt. 23:37–39), and that this city would be trodden down by the Gentiles until their time would be fulfilled (Luke 21:24). As sin and wickedness increase and the love of many grows cold, this period will culminate in judgment and usher in the kingdom (Matt. 24:9–28).

Jesus identified Himself as the ruler of this kingdom (Matt. 24:29–31). During His earthly life, He was identified as king on various occasions. The wise men looked for the one who was born King of the Jews (Matt. 3). After the feeding of the multitude, Jesus did not allow Himself to be recognized as king (John 6:15), but during His triumphal entry into Jerusalem He accepted the honors and acclaim usually accorded a ruler. In the judgment hall, Jesus assented to Pilate's statement that He was the king of the Jews (Matt. 27:11). Above the cross at the time of Jesus' crucifixion was inscribed "This is the King of the Jews" (Matt. 27:37).

After His death and resurrection Jesus spoke to His followers about the kingdom of God (Acts 1:1–11). Asked the direct question, "Will you at this time restore the kingdom to Israel?" He answered that the time of restoration was not for them to know. Heavenly messengers confirmed to the disciples the comforting words which Jesus had spoken assuring them of His return.

THE PURPOSE OF THE LAW OF LOVE

Jesus specifically related the law of love to man's entrance into the kingdom. In discussing the two great commandments in response to the question of eternal life, Jesus assured the lawyer that he would live if he loved God wholeheartedly and his neighbor as himself (Luke 10:25–29). The scribe, who pondered the same law of love, was assured that he was near the kingdom. Jesus repeatedly asserted that He had come to fulfill this law and that through His ministry and death God's love was manifested that whosoever would respond to Him would have eternal life.

Jesus before His ascension provided for the continual manifestation of God's love in this world through His disciples. "By this shall all men know that ye are my disciples, if ye have love one to another" (John 13:34). Mutual love for one another on the part of those who continue in love with Christ in the keeping of His commandments will continue to be a living witness to God's love in the lives of individuals. To the company of the committed, Jesus Christ said, "As the Father hath sent me, even so send I you" (John 20:20).